CIRCULAR WALKS

IN THE P

GW00360994

PA

20 WALKS OF 6 TO 10 MILES

Follow the Countryside code

1) Be safe and plan ahead and follow any signs
2) Keep dogs under control
3) Prevent uncontrolled moorland fires
4) Protect plants and animals, take your litter home
5) Leave gates and property as you find them
6) Consider other people
7) Beware mineshafts! Derbyshire alone has over 100,000 mine shafts. Keep away from depressions in the ground in the mining areas of the Peak District. Several of the walks in this book pass through mining areas, so stay on rights of way at all times.

Published by **Ashbourne Editions**
Ashbourne Hall, Cokayne Ave
Ashbourne, Derbyshire, DE6 1EJ England
Tel: (01335) 347349 Fax: (01335) 347303
e-mail: landmark@clara.net

13 ISBN: 978 1 873775 33 2

British Library Cataloguing in Publication Data: a catalogue
record for this book is available from the British Library.

Printed by: Cromwell Press Ltd, Trowbridge

Design & reproduction by: Michelle Prost

Front cover: Curbar Edge
Back cover: Doxy Pool, The Roaches
Opposite page: Cave Dale

CIRCULAR WALKS

IN THE PEAK DISTRICT

PAT TIDSALL

20 WALKS OF 6 TO 10 MILES

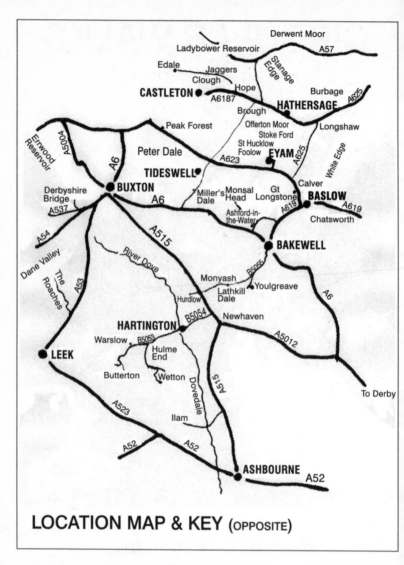

LOCATION MAP & KEY (OPPOSITE)

All the walks start at recognised car parks unless stated otherwise in the detailed walk descriptions.

Hanging Stone Walk 10

⟋	Roads	🌿🌳	Woods
⟋	Tracks: Drives	🪨	Rock Outcrops
↝	Railways	⊹	Church
◢	Trails	▲	Youth Hostel
⇗A	The Route	F B	Footbridge
∼	Rivers	C. P.	Car Park
◌	Lakes	P. H.	Public House: Inns

5

WALK INDEX

HARTINGTON AREA				
Walk 15	Hartington and The Dales	8 miles	3	57
Walk 16	Hulme End and Butterton	6¹/₂ mile	2★	60
Walk 17	Wetton and The Manifold Way	6¹/₂ miles	3★	64
HATHERSAGE AREA				
Walk 18	Offerton Moor and Derwent Heritage way	9¹/₂ miles	3	68
Walk 19	Stanage Edge and Redmires Reservoir	9 miles	4	72
TIDESWELL AREA				
Walk 20	Peter Dale and Miller's Dale	8¹/₂ miles	2	75

WALK INDEX

An explanation of terms used in addition to the map key:

1. All map references relate to the 1:25,000 Ordnance Survey maps of The Peak District [OL24 and OL1]. It may be helpful to have the touring map of "Peak District & Derbyshire" 1:100, 000 to locate the car parks. The maps in this book are only intended as a guide to the route, we consider it advisable always to carry the relevant O.S. map.

2. Parking is given with the Grid Ref. and in all but two walks is at a public car park and also the start of the walk. On two walks you will park on a minor road and a layby. Please take care when parking on the road.

3. Linear distance is given to the nearest $^1/_2$ mile and does not take into consideration the ascents and descents.

4. The approximate time given is for reasonably fit walkers based on walking 2 miles an hour. This can vary with weather conditions and the terrain. It does not allow for stops. Please ensure suitable footwear is worn.

5. Grades: 1: less than 300ft [91 metres]

        2: 300ft to 600ft [91 metres to 183 metres]

        3: 600ft to 1000ft [183 metres to 305metres]

        4: over 1000ft [305 metres]

6. The [*] indicates a section that may be difficult because of ascent, descent or terrain.

7. Stiles:- **S** – 1 to 10, **SS** – 10 to 20, **SSS** – over 20.

8. Refreshment and picnic areas are suggested but please bear in mind that they are not recommendations as the former can change hands and picnic areas may change.

    The countryside is not static and changes may have taken place between the research for these walks and their publication. Please note that the directions given in the route instructions are as you stand with your back to the stile or gate.

    Please read the details regarding lead mining at the beginning of the book.

Weather conditions in this area can change swiftly. The hills and upper moorlands can be much colder and windier than the dales and lowlands. Please always be aware of the latest weather conditions and have suitable equipment and clothing to cover all weathers.

We hope you will enjoy these longer walks as much as we did making them.

Acknowledgements

The author wishes to thank her husband, Peter, for all hiss assistance and encouragement in compiling this book along with members of her family; Karen, Ian and David and friends Christine, Janet and Allan.

She has been particularly lucky in arousing the interest of Roma Wilcock, whose love of walking has contributed greatly to the production of this book as well as being a good companion on many of the walks.

*Jaggers Clough
Walk 13*

WALK 1

Hurdlow And Monyash

High Peak Trail, Moscar Farm, Monyash, Limestone Way, Flagg, Pomeroy, High Peak Trail.

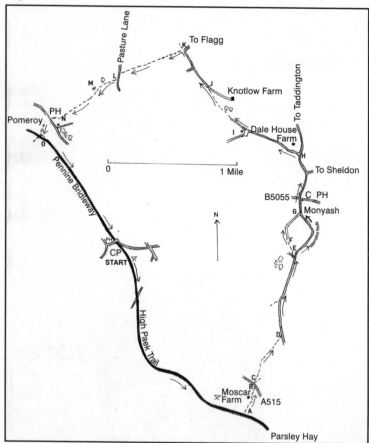

Map: Explorer OL24 White Peak
Parking: Hurdlow Trail Car Park SK 128659
Linear Distance: 7 miles

Approx. Time: 2³/₄ hours

Grade: 2

Paths: Trail, field paths and tracks

Stiles: SSS

Refreshments: Monyash, Pomeroy and The Royal Oak near the car park

Picnic: Near the car park and along the trail

Toilets: At the inns

Directions

From Ashbourne take the A515 road to Buxton. After just over 12 miles turn left to Longnor and Crowdecote. In about 400 metres turn left into the Hurdlow Trail car park.

Description

This is an easy walk for a breezy sunny day over an open area with wide reaching views. The trail at the start will give you a good leg stretch before crossing fields to the pretty village of Monyash. The return route follows part of the Limestone Way to Flagg. It would be advisable not to walk this route during the Flagg races at Easter time.

Route Instructions

1. With your back to the car park entrance, the buildings and the gate and bridge, walk in a southerly direction along the High Peak Trail.

2. After about ¹/₂ hour walking you will pass a small gate at the top of a bank on the left, this leads into a small picnic area. Just before Parsley Hay turn left off the trail at the footpath post. {A}

3. Cross the stile to walk up the field and over another stile. Follow the wall on the left. Cross the stile by the gate bearing right to cross another stile. Cross Moscar Farm drive and keep straight on passing the farm on the left before bearing left to follow the wall on the left. Cross the stile in the field corner. {B}

4. Turn left along the A515 for about 50 metres then cross the busy road to go down a bank and through a gateway [or over a stile] by the footpath post. {C}

5. Bear left aiming for the lower of two large trees by the wall ahead. Cross a squeeze stile under the tree. Bear right across the field corner to cross a way marked stile. Walk almost diagonally across the next long field crossing a line of rough ground and aiming for the stile in the opposite wall, which you cross.

6. Bear left across the next field corner crossing a stile then bear right towards and over a wooden stile. Follow the short path to the road. {D} Turn left along the road

for about ³/₄ mile, ignoring a path off left.

7. Just past a copse of trees up to your left turn left by the footpath post to go through a farm gate. [PLEASE NOTE: If you are following this walk in the summer or early autumn it would be advisable to stay on the road as part of the track into Monyash can become impassable]

8. Bear round to the right to go through a very small gate by the right hand farm gate. {E}

9. Walk up the field, crossing a small rock out-crop and aiming for the waymarked post ahead and the stile beyond it in the field corner. Cross this stile and turn right through a squeeze stile by a gate. {F}

10. Follow a walled grass track for about ¹/₄ mile. The track bends sharp right and is crossed by an old farm gate and stile. At this point it is rather over grown and impass-able in the summer! At the end of the track go through a gap or a squeeze stile then on down the field to cross a stile before walking down to the road. {G}

11. Turn left into Monyash. Cross the B5055, the inn and café are over to your right. Keep straight on along Chapel Street passing a small car park and the chapel. At the right turn to Sheldon keep straight on. After about ¹/₂ mile from the B5055 crossroads turn left at the Limestone Way footpath post and converted barns. {H}

12. Walk up the walled track passing the barns of Dale House Farm. After nearly ¹/₂ mile keep straight on with a wall on the right and ignoring a stile on the right and passing a stone barn on the left. {I}

13. Continue ahead following a path down the overgrown walled track. After just over 250 metres cross the stile ahead.

14. Bear right almost diagonally across the field to cross a wall stile above the field corner. Walk towards a small copse to cross another stile. Keep straight on following the wall on the left to join the Knotlow Farm drive. {J}

15. Walk along the drive to the road. Keep straight on, walking towards Flagg. Where the road bends sharp right into the village, continue straight on to go through the farm gate ahead, passing a gate on the left. {K}

16. Turn left and follow the wall on the left up three fairly large fields and crossing three stiles.

17. Turn left up Pasture Lane for a few metres then turn right over the stile. {L}

18. Follow the wall on the right up to a small stand of trees. Go through the gate ahead and keep straight on across the animal enclosure, passing the small, enclosed pens on your right and go through the next gate ahead of you.

19. Bear left up the field aiming for a building on the skyline and passing a dew pond

on the right. {M} Cross two stiles in the field corners and keep straight on up the field to cross another wall stile.

20. Bear slightly right aiming for a wall corner and to the right of the building and wood. {N}

21. Just past the wall corner go over a stile by the gateway and walk up the field veering away from the wall on the right. Cross a stile by the field corner.

22. Turn right for a few metres and opposite The Duke of York car park cross the busy A515. Cross the stile and bear left across the Pomeroy Nursery yard to go through the gate.

23. Follow the wall on the right that shortly bends round to the left. Immediately after passing the bridge over the trail turn right down the bank to cross the stile onto the High Peak Trail. [Pennine Bridleway]{O}

24. Turn left along the trail for about a mile back to the car park.

WALK 2

Ilam And Dovedale

National Trust Car Park, Ilam, Manifold Valley, Castern Hall, Hopedale, Stanshope, Hall Dale, Dovedale, Ilam.

Map: Explorer OL24 White Peak
Parking: Ilam Hall SK 131508
Linear Distance: 8 miles
Approx. Time: $3^1/2$ hours
Grade: 2
Paths: Dale and field paths and tracks
Stiles: SSS
Refreshments: Watts Russell Hopedale, Izaak Walton and The National Trust café at Ilam Hall [limited opening in the winter]
Picnic: Hall Dale
Toilets: Ilam Visitor Centre, Dovedale car park.

Directions

From Ashbourne take the A515 road to Buxton. In about $1^1/4$ miles turn left down the Thorpe, Ilam and Dovedale road. In two miles follow the road round to the left by The Dog and Partridge, to continue into Thorpe village before descending to the

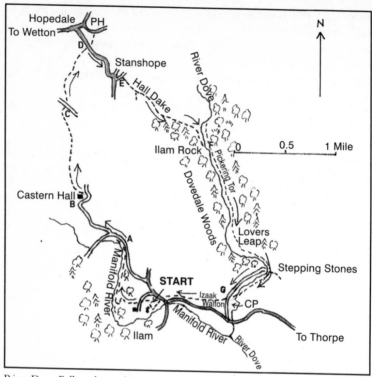

River Dove. Follow the road into Ilam village and at the monument turn right. Drive straight on along the National Trust driveway to the car park.

Walk Description

This walk takes you through some beautiful and refreshing countryside. The area is well known and rich with Derbyshire history. Izaac Walton chose it as his fishing centre for very good reasons and Dovedale has long been highly prized for its beauty and wildlife. Bird watchers abound as do holiday visitors.

Route Instructions

1. Leave the car park via the "Pedestrians this way" and the "Visitor Facilities" notices. Continue past the shop and Tea Rooms to follow the winding and partly stepped path down to the Manifold River.

2. Turn right to follow the riverside path keeping the meandering River Manifold

over to your left. Notice the Battle stone on the right. After about ½ mile cross a stile by a gate.

3. Continue ahead, still following the river, to cross a metal stile then a wooden stile and two small gates to reach the minor road. {A}

4. Turn left along the road for a few metres before taking the right fork. Walk up the Castern Hall driveway which winds its way quite steeply up hill for about ½ mile.

5. {B} Follow the metal fence on your left round Castern Hall then the waymarked route round the back of the hall to cross a cattle grid.

6. Bear left off the track at the footpath sign to follow the Wetton route. Cross a stile by a gate.

7. Keep to the farm track with a wall down on your left. Cross a stile by a gate. Bear right, away from the wall, to follow a grass path which has a slope down on the left and up on the right. Head for the right-hand gate on the skyline.

8. Cross the stile by the gate and keep straight on up the next field veering away from the wall on the right and passing a low rocky and grass mound on the left. Go through the gate ahead.

9. Keep straight on for a few metres then bear round to the right along a grass track with a wall on the left and old spoil heaps on the right. At a tall metal footpath post {C} cross two stiles and a track. [Instructions 7, 8, and 9 should take about 25 minutes]

10. Following the "Public Footpath to Hopedale" route bear left across the first field to go through a stile then keep straight on crossing three fields and stiles with walls on the left. In the fourth field, where the wall bends up left keep straight on to cross a stile in the field corner.

11. Continue ahead across the next field to go through a small gate then follow the wall close on your right down to the field corner where you cross a stile onto the road. {D} Turn right along the road into the hamlet of Stanshope. [If you need refreshments at The Watts Russell in Hopedale cross the road to walk down into the small dale where you turn left down to the road via a stile. Turn left along the minor road to Hopedale. To return walk up the steep path opposite the inn to join the Stanshope road where you turn left]

12. At Stanshope Hall follow the road round to the right and almost immediately turn left down a lane to Milldale. In about 70 metres turn right at the sign "Footpath to Dovedale via Hall Dale". {E}

13. Cross the field corner and go over a stile on your left then bear very slightly right to cross a gated stile near the field corner. Continue ahead keeping a wall on the right and passing a stile on the right. Cross another stile and a small gate.

14. Enter the National Trust Hall Dale area. Walk down this beautiful dry valley crossing two stiles. [It will take about 15 minutes]

15. On reaching the River Dove turn right over a wall stile. Follow the path to Ilam Rock where you cross the Dove to turn right below the towering limestone rocks of Pickering Tor. {F}

16. Enjoy the easy 20 minutes walking along the riverside path to the famous stepping stones. You will go through two gates one stile and climb one hill over Lovers Leap.

17. Cross the stepping stones to follow the driveway to the Dovedale car park. If the stones are flooded keep to the rocky path on the left bank of the river then cross the bridge.

18. {G} At the entrance to the car park turn right over the stile and bear left across the over flow car park to go up the steps, through the trees and over the stile.

19. Continue ahead across four fields, three stiles and one gate, passing the Izaak Walton Hotel. After the third stile, follow the track for about 100 metres then bear left down the bank to the road, pass through the small gate and turn right into Ilam.

20. At the monument turn right. Before reaching the main entrance into the grounds of Ilam Hall turn left at the "Church" sign then left again through a gate signed "Footpath to Church and Hall". Follow the driveway then turn right up a path by the church going through a small gate. At the top of the path cross the main drive to walk back into the car park.

WALK 3

Ashford-in-the-water And The Wye Valley

Churchdale Hall, Monsal Trail, Monsal Head, White Lodge Car Park, Taddington Field, Sheldon, Little Shacklow Wood, Ashford-in-the-Water.

Map: Explorer OL24 White Peak
Parking: Ashford-in-the-Water car park SK195698
Linear distance: $9^1/_2$ miles
Approx. Time: $4^1/_2$ hours
Grade: 3★
Paths: Tracks and woodland paths
Stiles: SS.
Refreshments: Sheldon, Ashford and Monsal Head
Picnic: Wye Valley and White Lodge Car Park
Toilets: Ashford and Monsal Head car parks.

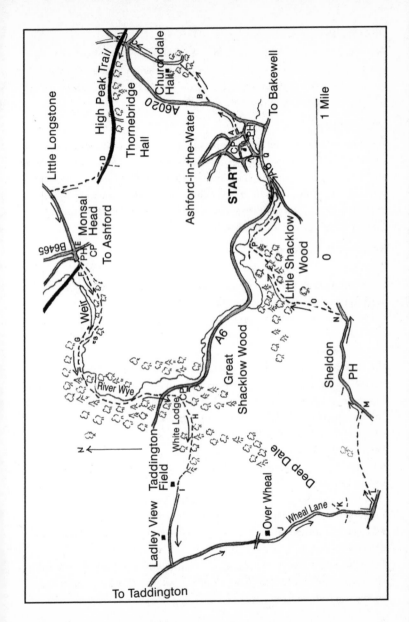

17

Directions

From Bakewell take the A6 Buxton road. In 1¹/₂ miles turn right at the A6020 Chesterfield and Sheffield sign. In a few metres turn left into Ashford-in-the-Water. As you enter the village keep straight on passing the inn and the church to turn right up Fennel Street. Turn right to follow the car parking signs.

Description

This walk covers a beautiful and attractive area of the county whilst being quite near centres of activity and population in Bakewell and Matlock. Deep valley paths give shade in the summer. Tracks, trails and lanes lead to pretty villages and extensive views over pleasing and dramatic countryside. After an acceptable amount of exercise you reach Monsal Head where the "batteries can be recharged!" Along the route you will see evidence of mining including Magpie Mine.

Route Instructions

1. Leave the car park to turn left immediately after the entrance [before you reach Fennel Street]. Walk along the village street passing the church on the right. At the road junction turn left and opposite The Ashford Arms turn left again up the Monsal Head road. In a few metres turn right along Hall End Lane. {A}

2. Go through a squeeze stile to follow a path up to the A6020 Chesterfield road and turn left up the pavement.

3. In about 350 metres and just before the two arrow bend signs turn right through a stile then a gate to walk up the rather steep path through the trees. {B} Cross a stile to keep straight on up the next two fields going over a fence stile and passing a stone barn over to the right. Cross a wall stile near a gateway.

4. Continue up the field passing Churchdale Hall on the left. Cross the stile ahead onto the drive and turn left.

5. Follow the drive for nearly ¹/₂ mile, passing Churchdale Hall and Lodge, to the road. {C}

6. Cross the road to walk along "Gt. Longstone Rowland" road and under the bridge. Immediately turn right on the Hassop road and then right again at the Monsal Trail sign. Follow a path up to the Trail. Turn right and walk along the Monsal Trail, passing Thornbridge Hall, for about ³/₄ mile.

7. {D} Near the end of the walkable part of the trail turn right over a wall stile. Keeping a wall close on the left walk down the field to go through a gate. Continue ahead crossing two fields and gates.

8. On reaching the road in Little Longstone turn left to walk through the village and on up to Monsal Head, just over $^1/_4$ mile.

9. Cross the B6465 at Monsal Head to walk in front of the Stable Inn and the café. {E} Go through the wall gap ahead [do not turn right] to walk down the limestone path onto the path above the dale, passing the "Ashford" sign. {F}

10. Walk down the fence edged path passing through two gates. After nearly $^1/_2$ mile you will pass the weir before crossing the footbridge over the River Wye.

11. Turn left to follow the partly wooded riverside route. {G} You will catch glimpses of the river along this 1 mile, gently undulating, wide path. Cross two stiles and walk across the A6.

12. Walk up to White Lodge car park in the trees. Pass the pay machine to walk up the surfaced path. After passing through a small gate look for the way-marked post up on the right, about 50 metres from the gate.

13. Turn right off the main path to walk up the less obvious steep rock strewn path on the Taddington route. Climb the low limestone outcrop to carry on up the rough grassy slope. Soon you will have an old wall and fence over to the left; do not veer too far away from them.

14. Cross a stile ahead of you and keep straight on for about 100 metres to turn left over and through a stile that is hidden from view until you are opposite it. {H}

15. Turn right up the wooded, steep-sided dale keeping an old wall and fence on the right. The first section is quite rocky underfoot but as you climb up the dale it soon opens out and the terrain is easier.

16. Near the top of the dale pass through a wide wall gap, the stile is over grown! Continue up the narrow rough field to cross a wall stile below Taddington Field. Bear right to go through a small gate.

17. {I} Turn left to follow the farm drive, passing Lodley View, for about $^1/_2$ mile to the road junction.

18. Turn left along the minor road for about $^3/_4$ mile, ignoring all turnings off it. Immediately after passing Over Wheal Farm the road becomes a track – Wheal Lane {J}. Follow this track, which has one very muddy short section, for nearly 1 mile to the secondary road. Towards the end of this track you will descend and ascend the top end of Deep Dale, {K} this is the least strenuous crossing of Deep Dale.

19. Turn left for about 100 metres then left again over a gated stile by the footpath post. {L}

20. Bear right to walk in more or less the same north-easterly direction across six fields and six stiles. At first aim for a stand of trees. In the fourth field keep the power

lines on your left aiming to the left of a fenced dew pond and in the sixth field bear left to the field corner.

21. {M} Turn left up the road to walk into Sheldon village. Pass the "Cock and Pullet" inn. Continue out of the village downhill and just after the last cottage on the left and at a left hand bend turn left by the footpath post. Go down and through a gated stile. {N}

22. Walk down the field aiming for the trees and a farm gate. Follow a wall on the left to go through a small gated stile, ignore the gate up to the right. Keep straight on to go through another gate into Little Shacklow Wood. {O}

23. Follow the rocky valley path down through the woods. Soon you will see a cave over to the right, before a steeper meandering descent. The path flattens out and is less rocky as you near the bottom of the wood. This woodland route is about ³/₄ mile.

24. Cross a stile by a gate to leave the wood. Walk down the field keeping a wall and the wood on the right. At the wall ahead turn right through a gateway. {P}

25. You now have the river and the A6 on the left. Cross a stile by a farm gate ahead. Follow the clear well-used riverside path with a fence on the right for about 375 metres [5 minutes]. Go through two gates and up a short track to the road. Turn left down the road to the A6 and turn right along the pavement.

26. {Q} Cross the busy A6 before the Chesterfield turn to walk over the sheep-wash bridge into Ashford-in-the-Water. Keep straight on passing the memorial on your right, to walk up Fennel Street. Pass the Cottage Tea Rooms and back to the car park.

WALK 4

Monsal Head, Cressbrook Dale And Foolow

Monsal Head Car Park, Viaduct and Monsal Trail, Cressbrook Dale, Wardlow Mires, Stanley House, Grindlow, Foolow, Housley, Longstone Moor, Little Longstone, Monsal Head.

Map: Explorer OL24 White Peak
Parking: Monsal Head SK185715
Linear distance: 9¹/₂ miles
Approx. Time: 4¹/₂ hours
Grade: 3
Paths: Dale paths and tracks, field and moorland paths

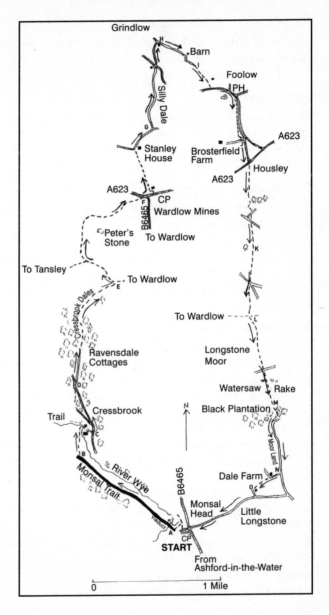

Grindlow

Barn

Foolow
PH

Silly Dale

A623

G

Stanley
House

Brosterfield
Farm

Housley

A623

A623

A623   CP
Wardlow Mines

F

B6465

Peter's
Stone

To Wardlow

K

To Tansley

To Wardlow

E

Cressbrook Dales

To Wardlow

L

Ravensdale
Cottages

Longstone
Moor

D

Watersaw   Rake

Cressbrook

Black Plantation

M

Trail

N

C

River Wye

B

Moor Land

Dale Farm

N

Monsal Trail

O

Monsal
Head

B6465

Little
Longstone

Viaduct

A

CP

START

From
Ashford-in-the-Water

0   1 Mile

21

Stiles: SSS

Refreshments: Monsal Head [Hobb's Café closed on Monday] and Foolow

Picnic: Top of Cressbrook Dale Instruction 7 and Longstone Moor

Toilets: Monsal Head Car Park

Directions

From Bakewell take the A6 Buxton road. In 1 1/2 miles turn right on the A6020 then left into Ashford-in-the-Water on the B6465 which almost immediately turns right signed Monsal Head. Follow this road for about 1¹/₂ miles. Turn left into the Monsal Head Car Park.

Description

Monsal Head, at the start of this walk is a famous view point overlooking the spectacular Monsal Dale and viaduct. After following the trail the route takes you down into Cressbrook Dale, the first part of which is a climb up through woodland then down into the open wide grassy section of the upper part of the dale. After the pretty village of Foolow the route is due south across fields and the open moorland of Longstone moor where you are rewarded with far reaching views of Kinder behind you and the rolling hills of the White Peak ahead.

Route Instructions

1. From the car park walk between the two parts of the Monsal Head Hotel. Turn left along the road to walk to the larger opening in the low stone wall opposite the café. Go through and turn right.

2. Descend the valley via shallow stone steps. A short way down turn left signed "Viaduct and Monsal Trail". {A} Continue downhill to the trail and turn right.

3. Cross the viaduct to continue along the Monsal Trail for nearly 1 mile. Just before the sealed off tunnel turn right through a gate. {B} The trail now contours the hillside. Ignore a path off left. Descend a steeply stepped path to cross a footbridge by the weir on the River Wye.

4. After crossing the river bear round to the right, leaving the Monsal Trail, to follow a fenced path round the converted mill buildings. At the road junction turn left. {C}

5. In a few metres bear right to walk up the road, signed "Cressbrook and Litton". In just over ¹/₄ mile bear right along the road to Ravensdale, which is a no through road route. {D} Pass the cottages to follow a narrow path by the footpath sign keeping a fence on the right and going through a gate at the end of the path.

6. Follow the main dale path through the woods and uphill, ignoring paths off left and

with an old wall down on the right. Cross a footbridge. At a fork of paths bear right uphill, the path now starts to climb up away from the river.

7. {E} At the top of the dale by an English Nature sign bear left to descend back down into Cressbrook Dale on a clear path. Walk along the grassy dale for about ³/₄ mile, ignoring the path on the left. Notice the impressive Peter's Stone up on the right. At the end of the dale keep a wall close on the right. Go through a gate across the path. {F} Walk behind a building then in front of a house [this is a private dwelling and driveway as well as the footpath so please take care].

8. Turn right along the A623 crossing the entrance to the Wardlow road. Opposite the car park and the transport café turn left to cross the road to the footpath sign and farmyard.

9. Walk down the short drive to turn left following the F P route round the barns. Go through a gate into the field behind the barns.

10. Cross the next two fields keeping a wall on the left and crossing two stiles. In the third field bear left uphill aiming for the field corner and Stanley House at the top of the field. Cross the stile by the gate.

11. Turn right to walk along the track passing Stanley House on the right. In about 375 metres follow the track round a left hand bend. {G} Continue up the walled grassy track, walking parallel to Silly Dale, for nearly ¹/₂ mile.

12. At the road junction keep straight on up the minor road into Grindlow. At a left hand bend turn right by the building by the Footpath sign. {H}

13. Follow the track and at a large barn on the left and a gate ahead turn right . The track now becomes somewhat overgrown leaving only a narrow path. At the end of the track go through a squeeze stile. {I}

14. Keep straight on to cross the stile ahead. Walk across the paddock passing a large house to your left, [this area is part of the grounds to the house so please take care]. Cross a driveway to go over a low squeeze stile. Bear right across the field to cross a double stile.

15. Turn left down the road into Foolow. Walk past the green, the duck pond and opposite The Bulls Head turn right on the Wardlow Middleton road.

16. Walk along the pavement on the right hand side of the road for about ¹/₄ mile. The pavement will bring you down to the entrance to Brosterfield Farm where you bear right {J} and walk down the road to the A623. [Do not go along the Brosterfield drive].

17. Cross this busy road to Housley House and cross the wall stile on the right. Turn left passing the house on the left [again take care as this is part of the garden].

18. Cross the fence stile to follow the wall on the left then cross another stile by a gate. Bear diagonally right up the next field to go over another stile, cross the next field to pass through a flapped stile in the right hand field corner.

19. Walk past a wood on the left then bear right away from crossing the small field to go over a fence stile in the field corner. Cross the farm drive to go over a wall stile. Bear right across the field ahead to go through a wall stile.

20. Cross the minor road and go over a low ladder stile. Walk up the larger field aiming about 100 metres to the left of a large tree [about $3/4$ of the way along the wall over to the left]. {K} Cross a wall stile. Bear right across the field corner aiming about 50 metres to the left of the same tree, cross the stile.

21. Continue in the same southerly direction crossing fields, stiles, broken walls and gates which you can see ahead of you, also a track.

22. Cross the road and the stile by the footpath post. Keep straight on in the same direction to cross three fields and stiles. In the third field there are old open cast lead mine hollows so take care to follow the path across the middle of the field.

23. {L} On reaching open moorland bear slightly left following a narrow undulating path which shortly climbs up through the heather. In nearly $1/2$ mile pass a footpath sign and walk downhill. Cross a raised track to go down a bank between the fences round Watersaw Rake and then continue up through the heather. Soon you will descend towards Black Plantation wood.

24. Cross a stile by a gate and turn left. {M} Follow the steep winding path through the wood. Near the end of the wood go down steps, cross a track and bear right down to and through a gate.

25. Turn right down the road. In just over $1/4$ mile take the first right turn to Dale Farm. {N} Walk up the lane passing Dale Farm and where the lane bends right cross the stile on the left.

26. Follow the wall on the left to cross another stile. Just past a house on the left cross a stile by a gate. {O} Walk down the track to the road.

27. Turn right along the road through Little Longstone to walk back to Monsal Head. [About $2/3$ of a mile]

WALK 5

Monyash And Lathkill Dale

Moor Lane Car Park near Youlgreave, Limestone Way via One Ash Grange to Monyash, Bagshaw Dale, Lathkill Dale, Meadow Place Grange, Moor Lane Car Park.

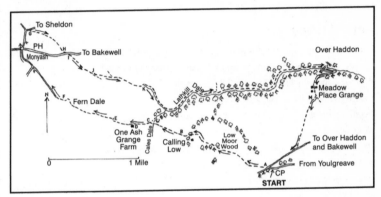

Map: Explorer OL24 White Peak.

Parking: Moor Lane Car Park SK194644

Linear distance: 9 miles

Approx. Time: 4^1/$_4$ hours

Grade: 2*

Paths: Field paths, tracks and limestone dale paths

Stiles: SSS

Refreshments: In Monyash

Toilets: Instruction 16

Picnic: Lathkill Dale

Directions

From Bakewell take the A6 south. Pass the entrance to Haddon Hall then turn right to Youlgreave passing through Alport. Drive into Youlgreave passing the church and The Bulls Head on the left. At the tall circular well ahead bear right then turn right at a T-junction of village roads. Drive up the narrow "quiet" Moor Lane for about a mile. Turn left into the car park.

Description

A walk across open fields with far reaching views above the dales takes you to the pretty village of Monyash. From here you follow Lathkill Dale where the scenery varies from gentle open fields to narrow rocky gorges to wide tree-lined paths below the towering limestone cliffs. The return to the car park is across open fields.

Limestone can be very slippery when wet so it is advisable to follow this route in dry weather.

Route Instructions

1. Leave the car park via the main entrance and turn left. In about 130 metres cross the secondary road to go over the gated stile signed "Monyash". {A}

2. Walk diagonally left across the field. Cross the wall stile then cross the corner of the next field to go over another gated wall stile.

3. Follow the well defined path across the middle of the large field walking in a North West direction. Cross a fence stile and continue in the same direction to go through a small gate and then follow the path through Low Moor Wood. Go through the gate in the wood corner.

4. Walk diagonally across the next field towards Calling Low Farm. Go through a small gate to keep straight on for a few metres before going through a gate on the left.

5. Walk through the trees passing through three swing gates. Bear right across the field corner to go through another small gate by the footpath sign. {B} Bear slightly left following the Cales Dale route down the middle of the next three fields and going through three gates.

6. Walk down the limestone steps into Cales Dale. Cross the stile and bear left up the short steep path ignoring a path off left. At the T-junction of paths turn left {C} to walk below the limestone cliffs on the right, this path is very rocky and steep in places.

7. Go through a small gate and continue ahead across the field towards One Ash Grange Farm. Cross a stile at the top of a short flight of steps by the black barn. {D}

8. Follow the farm track between the barns before passing a cave, possibly used for cooling cheese, and medieval piggeries on your right. Continue to follow the track as it bends round to the right through a gateway.

9. At the top of the track go through a gateway and turn left. {E} Walk up the field keeping the wall close on the left. Just before the field corner cross a stile on the left and turn right.

10. Follow the wall on the right to cross two fields with one gate and one stile. Cross the top end of Fern Dale and bear right up the field to go over the wall stile ahead

into the "National Trust Fern Dale" area.

11. Turn left and in a few metres go through the gate on the left to enter a walled track. {F}

12. Follow this track for about $^1/_2$ mile. At the road junction turn right to walk into Monyash.

13. Cross the B5055 road [Bakewell, Buxton, Ashbourne], the Bulls Head and café are off to the right. Walk past the chapel on the right and a car park on the left. At the bottom of the hill turn right signed "Sheldon".

14. In a few metres turn right through a squeeze stile by a metal gate and the footpath sign to Lathkill Dale. {G} Walk through a small field to cross a gated stile.

15. Keep straight on along the shallow muddy Bagshaw Dale going through one gate, one gap and two stiles. In about $^1/_4$ mile join a wider clearer track to cross a stile by the farm gate. Immediately turn left down a narrow path to the road. {H}

16. Cross the road to the toilets and turn left then almost immediately turn right through a gate into Lathkill Dale. {I}

17. At first you follow a wide grass path before entering a narrow rocky section of the dale {J} with steep limestone cliffs. Eventually you reach a large cavern on the right, {K} from which the River Lathkill flows after a period of heavy rain. The Dale path gradually becomes wider and more wooded. This is a very peaceful easy section of the dale.

18. At the end of the dale [about 3 miles] join the minor road from Over Haddon via the second gate and turn right to cross the footbridge. {L}

19. Turn left to follow a wide steep track uphill and round a right-hand bend. Pass through a farm gate at the top of the track.

20. Turn left across the field to Meadow Place Grange. Go through the farm gate then across the yard and over a wall stile. Walk up a short muddy track, then follow a wall close on the right ignoring the footpath to Youlgreave.

21. When you reach the next footpath sign {M} to Middleton turn left up the field aiming for a short post. Cross the wall stile ahead.

22. Bear slightly left to cross the middle of the next two fields and crossing two stiles.

23. Turn right up the road for nearly $^1/_2$ mile before turning left back to the car park.

WALK 6

Calver And Great Longstone

Calver, Coombs Dale, Black Harry Gate, Longstone Edge, Great Longstone, Monsal Trail, Rowland, Deep Rake, Calver.

Map: Explorer OL24 White Peak.

Parking: In Calver SK238748

Linear distance: $8^1/2$ miles

Approx. Time: $4^1/4$ hours

Grade: 4★

Paths: Mainly tracks with some field paths

Stiles: SS easy

Refreshments: The White Lion in Great Longstone [closed on Tuesdays] and the café in Calver

Picnic: Instructions 9 and 21

Toilets: At the inns.

Directions

From Baslow take the A623 Stockport road. In just over 2¼ miles, park where convenient and safe in Calver. The walk starts at the crossroads of the A623, the A625 and the B6001.

Description

There is a definite open air feeling on this walk after a gentle "conversational walk" up Coombs Dale. In addition you will see many examples of the early mining activities of the area as well as present day quarrying, especially at Black Harry Gate. Calver, mentioned in the Domesday Book, repays a stroll round.

Route Instructions

1. Walk along the A623 towards Stoney Middleton passing the factory shop on the left. After 400 metres from the crossroads turn left at the footpath and "Private Road". {A}

2. Ignoring all side paths walk up the 2mile gradually ascending track of Coombs Dale, the first part of which is surfaced.

3. Pass by a gate near the quarry workings of Black Harry Gate. {B} At the crossing of tracks and quarry roads pass a farm gate on the left, cross the wide quarry "road" and go through a small metal gate on the left.

4. Walk up the short, wide walled track, ignore the bridleway on the left to go through the small gate ahead.

5. Follow a wall close on the left as you walk up the field. Go through another gate. Continue up a wide fenced and walled track to go through the next gate. Keep straight on with a wall still on the left.

6. As you near the quarry road of High Rake go through the waymarked farm gate on your left {C} and turn right to go through another farm gate. Cross the wide track to pass through waymarked posts.

7. Keep straight on across the rough grass area to cross a stile ahead [ignore the stiles over to your left]. Walk down the steep grass slope into a narrow V-shaped valley. Descend this valley on an uneven steep path that could be slippery in wet weather.

8. Cross a track, ignoring a stile on the left and turn right to follow a narrow path [not the track]. This easier path crosses the hilside before descending more steadily to a fence stile. {D}

9. Cross the stile and here you will see the "picnic" bench with far reaching southward views. Keep straight on down and across the field to go through a small gate.

10. Turn right to walk round the rock outcrop, first with a wall on the right then through a wide moat-like area. {E} Soon you will see two paths bearing up right, follow either of these paths to go through a gate.

11. Bear right across the field to go through a squeeze stile in the field corner. Bear right again down to the bottom right hand corner of the field where you cross a stile by a gate.

12. Walk down the walled track to turn right along the road. Follow the road, passing the church, to the T-junction in Great Longstone. [There is a short cut through the churchyard]

13. {F} Cross the village road to footpath sign on the left of The White Lion. Walk up the alleyway between the houses to cross a stile. Pass the playing fields and cross the next road to keep straight on along a hedged and walled path by the houses. Turn left along the next road passing Furnall Avenue and in a few metres turn right by the footpath post. At the end of a short track go through a stile by a gate. [This area could be quite muddy] {G}

14. Bear left to a wall corner and continue in the same direction for a few metres to the gated stile in the fenced and hawthorn field boundary ahead. Cross the stile bearing right across the field corner to cross the next gated stile.

15. Walk diagonally down the large tree dotted field aiming for the bottom right hand corner. As you approach the wall and the trail on the right you will see a footpath sign before you reach the field corner. Cross the stile by this footpath sign. {H}

16. Turn right up to the Monsal Trail then turn left along the trail. After about $^1/_2$ mile turn left at a crossing of paths {I} to cross a field to the A6020 and the Toll House.

17. Go through a farm gate and turn left along the road for a few metres, then cross the road to go over the stile by the footpath post.

18. Head straight up the large field aiming for a wall and a copse of trees and following the small waymarked posts. At the top of the field follow the high wall close on the right. Cross three stiles and at the end of the wall cross the stile on the right and turn left down the track to the road.

19. {J} Cross the road diagonally left to walk into Rowland. Follow the road through the hamlet. At the "Unsuitable for Motor Vehicles" notice keep straight on. The first part of the track is surfaced.

20. Stay on the main track for nearly a mile ignoring all side paths. Just after the second cattle grid follow the main track as it bends round to the left passing the "Protected Site"

Ancient Monuments notice. Turn right passing the telegraph poles on your right.

21. {K} Cross a fence stile ahead. Walk down a path to join a wider path. Follow this path as it winds across the open rough grassy area, ignoring the right hand fork, before reaching a sunken gorse stretch.

22. Cross the stile by the farm gate. {L} Keep straight on following the field boundaries on your right. Go through two small gates then walk down a walled track. Go through a small gate by a farm gate, you now have a wall only on the left and the path swings round to the right. {M}

23. Cross a stile to walk down to the road via a squeeze stile. Turn left back to the crossroads in Calver.

WALK 7
Chatsworth And The Edges

Baslow, Chatsworth Park, The Hunting Tower, Dobb Edge, Birchen Edge Wellington's Monument, Baslow.

Map: Explorer OL24 White Peak.
Parking: Baslow car park Nether End Grid Ref SK258722
Linear distance: 7 miles
Approx. Time: 3 _ hours
Grade: 3*
Paths: Woodland, moorland, edges and parkland
Stiles: S
Refreshments: Baslow, Robin Hood, Chatsworth.
Picnic: Wellington's Monument
Toilets: Near the car park

Directions

From the junction of the A619 and A623 in Baslow, take the Chesterfield /Sheffield Road to Nether End Baslow. After passing the Cavendish Hotel on the right take a right fork off the main road to turn right into the car park.

Description

This walk is a "must". It combines beauty, grandeur, history and dignity as well as being a reasonably easy walk after you have climbed up to the Hunting Tower. There are

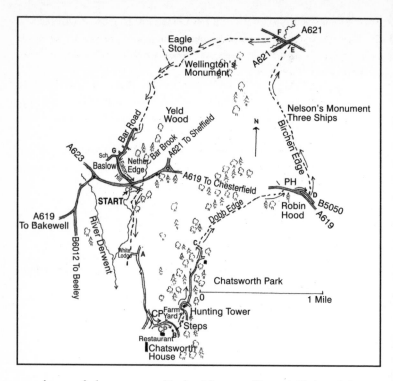

a number or refreshment stops and in the right season [Easter to Christmas] the very interesting Chatsworth House and gardens to visit.

Route Instructions

1. Leave the car park via the main entrance and turn right to cross the bridge over Bar Brook. Turn right again to follow a track passing cottages and going through a stile by the left-hand gate. Continue along the track to go through the Cannon Kissing Gate into the park.

2. Keep straight on following a well-used path to join a surfaced path. When you reach White Lodge, in about 500 metres, turn left up the short tree-lined estate road. At the T-junction turn right to follow the estate road. {A}

3. After about ¹/₂ mile at a fork of roads take the left hand fork to walk past the car park that is on the left. At the next junction of estate roads turn left to walk between the two parts of the car parking area. The restaurant and craft shops are over to your

right. Continue to follow the estate road as it swings round to the left aiming for the "Farmyards" and the "Adventure Playground".

4. Cross the cattle-grid, then follow the estate road as it bends round to the right following the "Stand Wood Walks" route and passing the farmyard on your left. In about 100 metres, opposite the first building and woodyard on the right, turn left by the low-level waymarked signs. {B}

5. Walk up a narrow woodland path to cross a track and continue up a winding path, crossing a stream and walking round a large yew tree to the steps.

6. Climb the steps to the Hunting Tower. [Over 140 steps]

7. Turn left to follow the estate road round the tower and at a crossing of roads turn left signed "Robin Hood". Follow this surfaced road for just over $^1/_4$ mile and where the road bends right up to a large barn keep straight on along a farm track.

8. Just before a gate turn left to follow a wall on the right. Cross the high wall stile and turn right. {C} Walk to the wall ahead, then follow it down the moorland.

9. From here you can see Nelson's Monument and "Three Ships". The path soon veers left down to and over another high wall stile. Keep straight on up the field to walk along the concessionary path across Dobb Edge. Cross the stile in the field corner.

10. Follow the narrow, winding, rocky and undulating path crossing two stiles. At the end of the Edge cross a ladder stile.

11. Bear left downhill following the waymarked signs, cross a track to follow the "Robin Hood" route. Continue down steps then across a footbridge before climbing a flight of steps to the road.

12. Cross the busy A619 and turn right. In about 200 metres turn left along the B road passing the Robin Hood Inn and the car park. In a few metres and just past a house on the left leave the road to turn left by the house drive. Walk up the short track on your right to go through a small gate on to access land. {D}

13. Keep straight on up the wide steps to walk parallel to a wall on your left. Ignore all smaller paths off right. Soon you will lose the wall on the left. As you gradually climb the rocky path bears up right towards the gritstone outcrops of Birchen Edge.

14. Follow the rock-strewn path below the edge. Nearing the northern end of Birchen Edge the path veers off left down through the heather and bracken before crossing a marshy area that can be very wet in places.

15. At the end of the moorland cross the stile and turn left to cross the A621. {E} Walk up the minor road opposite. At the top of the hill go through the small gate on the left and immediately turn right onto the track by the Access Land sign. {F}

16. Follow the track with the high wall on the right. This is the ancient "CHESTER-

FIELD ROADE", as you will see on a stone pillar ahead. Where the wall ends, keep straight on to Wellington's Monument. This is a favourite picnic spot. The highland cattle you may well see along this route are said to be very friendly and placid.

17. From the monument continue along the track for about another 150 metres to a T-junction of tracks where you turn left. Notice the Eagle Stone off to your right.

18. Follow the wide stony track downhill to go through a gate. Continue down the walled and hedged track for nearly ¹/₂ mile to meet a surfaced track that leads into Bar Road.

19. Walk down Bar Road, ignoring roads off left and right until you reach a grass island at the junction of School Lane and Bar Road. {G} Turn left to walk down Eaton Hill road to the A619. Cross the main road back to the car park.

WALK 8
White Edge And Longshaw Estate

Curbar Gap Car Park, White Edge, Longshaw Estate, The Grouse Inn, Froggatt Edge, Curbar Edge.

Map: Explorer OL24 White Peak
Parking: Curbar Gap SK262747
Linear distance: 8 miles
Approx. Time: 3¹/₄ hours
Grade: 2
Paths: Moorland and estate roads
Stiles: S
Refreshments: The National Trust café at Longshaw:- Opening times: 10.30am. Nov-Mar, weekends only; Mar-Jun & Sep-Nov, Wed-Sun; Jun-Sep, daily The Grouse Inn
Picnic: The Edges with wonderful views
Toilets: Longshaw

Directions

From Baslow take the A623 Stockport and Manchester road. In 1¹/₂ miles turn right to Curbar and in a few metres bear off right up Curbar Lane signed "Curbar Village". Follow this steep uphill road for about 1 mile, passing lay-bys on the left. At the top of the hill turn left into the pay and display car park.

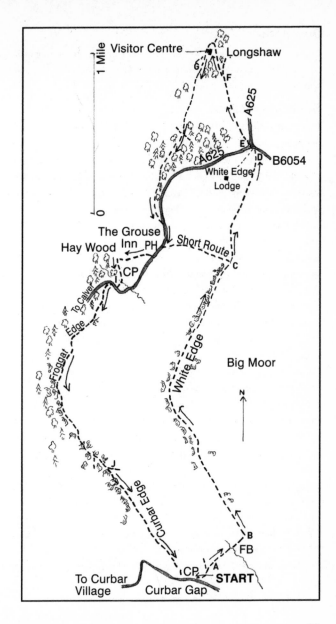

Description

This is easily one of our favourite walks. The open ruggedness and long views are conducive to bringing peace and happiness. Here the forces of nature in this world of ours are very positive and uplifting.

Route Instructions

1. Leave the car park with the road on your right, crossing the entrance. Go through the gate to enter the "Eastern Moors Estate".

2. Keep straight on for about 100 metres to a wall corner on the left and at this point leave the wall to keep straight on. [Do NOT bear round to the left] {A}

3. Continue down the moorland track aiming for the steep slope ahead. Cross a wooden bridge to climb the only steep slope on the walk.

4. {B} Turn sharp left at the wall corner signed "Longshaw". Shortly bear right away from the wall up onto the moors.

5. Follow the concessionary path along White Edge for 2 miles ignoring all side paths. In about 45 minutes you will pass through a wide wall gap. {C} At this point you can turn left down the moors to The Grouse Inn, this would give you a 5^1/$_2$ mile walk. To continue on to Longshaw keep straight on.

6. On reaching a fence on the left keep straight on ignoring the stile. Follow the line of the fence down to the road where you cross the wall stile. {D}

7. Turn left, crossing the road, then cross the grass-island and the road junctions aiming for the white estate gate over to the right. Go through the small gate by the white gate into the National Trust area of "Wooden Pole". {E}

8. Keep straight on along a wide grass path where there is a drop on your left and a high bank on the right. In nearly ^{1}/$_2$ mile you will see another white gate leading into open woodland. Walk to this gate and go through the small gate on the right of it. {F}

9. Follow the path through the open woodland to walk behind Longshaw House. Take a left-hand path to the Visitor Centre and café.

10. Turn right crossing the driveway to go down a short path then turn left. Walk along the path below the house. Go through two small gates under the yew trees, ignoring the path to the right.

11. {G} Follow the wide shale estate path, passing through a small gate about ^{1}/$_2$ way along, for 1^1/$_4$ miles to the A625.

12. Turn right down the road and just past The Grouse Inn turn right over a stile. {H}

13. Walk down three fields passing through a gate then aiming for a small gate in the

wall ahead. Go through this small gate and turn left.

14. Follow the path through the woods passing a car park on your left. Walk downhill to cross a stream then on up a steep bank to the road.

15. Turn right then cross the busy road to go through a gateway by the farm gate. {I}

16. Walk up the wide track to enter the birch wood. In about ¹/₂ mile go through a small gate. Continue along Froggatt and Curbar Edges. When you reach a divide in the path {J} [about 1¹/₄ miles] take the right-hand fork staying on the main edge route. After about 2 miles you will pass through a gate to keep straight on across a small embankment. Follow the path with the wall on the left back to the car park.

WALK 9

Errwood Reservoir And Derbyshire Bridge

Errwood Reservoir Dam, Bunsal Cob, Wild Moor, Goyt's Moss, Goyt's Clough Quarry, Derbyshire Bridge, Cat & Fiddle, Stake Side, Errwood Reservoir.

Map: Explorer OL24 White Peak.

Parking: Errwood Reservoir Car Park SK 013757

Linear distance: 7¹/₂ miles

Approx. Time: 3¹/₂ hours

Grade: 2

Paths: Moorland paths and tracks and minor roads

Stiles: None

Refreshments: The Cat & Fiddle on the A537

Picnic: Four marked areas along the Errwood Reservoir and Goyt's Clough

Toilets: Near Bunsal Cob and Derbyshire Bridge car park.

Directions

From the centre of Buxton take the A5004 Whaley Bridge road and in 2¹/₄ miles take the first turn left after leaving Buxton. Follow this minor road for 1¹/₂ miles down to the reservoirs. Just after crossing between them turn left then immediately right into the car park.

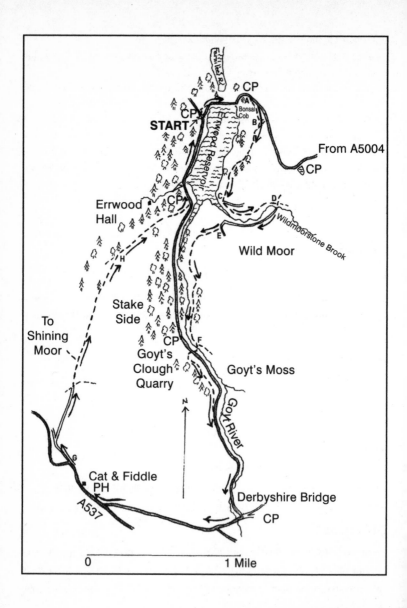

CP

Errdes R.

CP

START

Bonsall
Cob

A

B

From A5004

CP

Errwood Hall

CP

C

D

E

Wildmoorstone Brook

Wild Moor

To Shining Moor

H

Stake Side

CP
Goyt's Clough Quarry

F

Goyt's Moss

N

Goyt River

G

Cat & Fiddle PH

A537

Derbyshire Bridge

CP

0   1 Mile

38

Description

The moorland on either side of the Goyt River and the Errwood Reservoir offer stunning views on a clear day. The climbs up onto the moors are gradual and on the whole the paths are clearly defined and signed. There are some boggy stretches at instruction 8 so it would be advisable to follow this route after a period of dry weather. There are a number of inviting picnic spots in the Goyt valley.

Route Instructions

1. Leave the car park via the main entrance and turn left along the road. In a few metres at the road junction turn right taking the Fernilee Reservoir path down to the road. [Not through the small gate]

2. Walk back along the reservoir dam road and continue first round a left-hand bend then a right-hand bend. Opposite the small car park and toilets turn right by a plaque under the pine tree. {A} [Not very obvious]

3. Walk up a short, steep bank round Bunsal Cob, then continue ahead with the wood on Bunsal Cob behind you. At a crossing of paths keep straight on down a steep path through the wood. Join a wider path ahead and turn right. {B}

4. In a few metres cross a broken wall on the left to continue in the same direction. Join another path and turn right again to walk towards and through a wooded area.

5. Follow a wall on the left that you will soon lose as you cross moorland and broken walls.

6. In about ³/₄ mile from Bunsal Cob you will come to a junction of paths and a bench overlooking the reservoir. [A good coffee stop!] {C} Take the second path on the left, by the footpath sign, to follow a wide path with the reservoir inlet down on the right.

7. In about ¹/₄ mile cross a footbridge on the right {D} to follow the Goyt's Clough Quarry sign. Stay on the track for just over ¹/₄ mile, passing through one gate and having a wall on the right for the last few metres, until you reach a sign post. {E} Leave the track to turn right down a narrow path with a wall on the right.

8. Cross a footbridge and on up the slope still with the wall on the right for another 200 metres. Pass through a wall gap and continue in the same direction with the wall now up on the left. As you cross the moorland the bracken gives way to a more open, rather boggy area with some stretches crossed via duck-boards.

9. In just over ¹/₂ mile from the bridge [inst. 8] you will see the car park at Goyt's Clough Quarry and the small stone packhorse-bridge down to the right.

10. Walk down to and across the bridge then up to the road. {F} Cross the road to the signpost to Stake Side and Shining Tor.

11. Follow the wide grass path as it bends round to the left below the picnic area and then bends right by a waymark sign. Walk parallel to the road down on the left for about ¼ mile. When this path joins the road turn right. Follow the minor road for 1½ miles to Derbyshire Bridge.

12. Turn right up another minor road for a mile. Walk by the very busy A537 for about ¼ mile passing the **Cat & Fiddle**. [A good lunch stop]

13. Where the main road bends left keep straight on to follow a track. {G} In 300 metres take the right-hand fork and continue up the track for another ¼ mile. Ignore the routes off right to keep straight on through a small gate.

14. Follow the wall close on the left for about ¾ mile across the moorland. At a signpost and a small gate on the left turn RIGHT. {H}

15. Walk down Stake Side going through a gate. Near the bottom of the slope cross a wide path to go through a gateway then on down through a wood to the car park.

16. Turn left to walk along the reservoir road for about ½ mile back to the car.

WALK 10
The Roaches And The Dane Valley Way

Rockhall, The Roaches, Bearstone Rock, Hanging Stone, Danebridge, Dane Valley Way, Gradbach Woods, Shaw House.

Map: Explorer OL 24 White Peak,

Parking: Below The Roaches SK 004622 during the week; Park & Ride from Tittesworth Reservoir Visitor centre at weekends & Bank holidays.

Linear distance: 9½ miles

Approx. Time: 5½ to 6 hours

Grade: 4*

Paths: Ridge, dale and woodland; mainly rocky

Stiles: SS

Refreshments: The Tea Rooms just before the parking area below The Roaches [open: 9am-5.30pm; closing 4pm winter. The Ship Inn Wincle [250 metres from Danebridge; closed Monday]

Picnic: Anywhere between instruction 2 and 16

Toilets: None

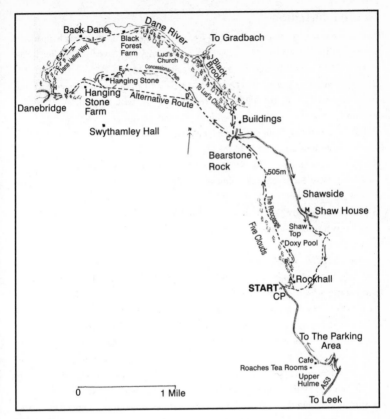

Directions

From Buxton take the A53 Leek road for nearly $8^{1}/_{2}$ miles. Take the second turn right to Upper Hulme. Follow the winding steep road, taking the left fork, down into and through the village. After about $^{3}/_{4}$ mile you will see parking areas at the side of the narrow road. The walk starts at the bus stop on the left hand side of the road.

Description

An invigorating walk across the gritstone edges of the western Peak District, where the views on all sides are very grand. The return route is in great contrast, being along the peaceful enclosed valley of the Dane River, before a steep climb up through woodland to the open moorland.

Route Instructions

1. At the bus stop go through the small gate and turn right up the gravelled path. In about 200 metres turn left up to the old stone buildings in the woods. [Rockhall] Pass Don Whillans memorial hut. Go through a wall gap. {A}

2. Keep straight on passing Rockhall on your right to climb the very steep rock and stone stepped path. At the top of the steps turn left to walk below the higher rock outcrops up on your right, then through a wooded area for about 300 metres.

3. {B} Turn right to climb the next rocky, partly stepped, steep slope. At the top turn left. You now have an old wall on the left for a short way.

4. Follow the well used rocky path across The Roaches. In about 400 metres you will pass Doxy Pool. After about 30 minutes walking you will reach the minor road near Bearstone Rock.

5. Just before the road take a short right hand fork to cross the road then up shallow steps to go through a squeeze stile then a small gate ahead back onto the Access Land. {C}

6. Follow a wall on the left for just over ¹/₂ mile and at a sign post take the Concessionary path {D} to keep straight on. You will go through two small gates. In about ³/₄ mile at another sign post turn left through a small gate signed "Swythamley". In a few metres turn right over a wall stile and through a gate signed "Hanging Stone". {E}

7. Bear slightly left across the tussock grass field to cross the gate and stile ahead. If you wish to see the hanging stone turn left at the waymarked post and return to the grass path as the route down directly from the stone is **very** steep. Continue down the grass path for a few metres then bear round to the left {F} passing the Hanging Stone up on the left and aiming for the clear shale track way below the stone.

8. Turn right along the shale track for about 300 metres passing Hangingstone Farm. Cross the stile on the left and bear right across the sloping field to cross another stile. Keep straight on passing a standing stone in the middle of the field.

9. As you descend the field aim for the wood on the right then follow the woodland boundary for a few metres before crossing a stile into the woods. {G}

10. Follow a clear path down through the woods. When you reach a waymarked post keep straight on following the concessionary route. Leave the woodland path via steps and a fence stile.

11. {H} Turn right to follow the Gradbach route. [If you wish to visit Danebridge and a pub in Wincle turn left]

12. The next section follows the undulating Dane Valley Way for 2 miles. At first the route is by the river then bears up right to cross a stile following a path through the

bluebell woods. After leaving the wood via a stile the path crosses the hillside passing Back Dane and following a wider track for a short way before leaving it {I} on the left at a bend. The route now winds up through the gorse bushes before crossing a stile and continuing ahead. A little further on, after crossing a bridge and a stile, the route follows a wide fenced grass track, with gates, to pass Black Forest Farm. Two more stiles are crossed before the path enters a wood where the River Dane is now down a steep gully on the left. At the footpath post the route continues ahead above the river.

13. At the end of the 2 miles you will notice a footbridge {J} over Black Brook down to the left and a footpath post, this is where you leave The Dane Valley Way. Keep straight on [not signed], at the top of a short climb turn left at a T-junction of paths. Black Brook is still down on the left.

14. At the next signpost follow the Roaches End route. Climb steeply up the undulating Gradbach Woods path. After about ¹/₂ mile you reach another footpath post where you keep straight on ignoring the Lud Church route. {K}

15. Cross a small valley to continue up a rocky woodland path. Soon you will leave the woods to have a wall on the left and a building over to the left. Climb gradually across the moors keeping the wall on the left. Eventually cross a stile and immediately turn left through a squeeze stile. [See instruction 5]

16. At this point you can retrace your outward route across The Roaches or:-

17. {L} Turn left up a minor unfenced road. Follow this road for nearly 1 ¹/₄ miles, passing Shawside. Just after a cattle grid and before Shaw House leave the road to turn right up a shale track. {M}

18. Just before a barn and a farm gate turn left over the stile. Walk below Shawtop to cross another stile.

19. Follow the path across the moor keeping the fence on the right. Cross a fence stile and turn right to keep the fence close on the right. In a few metres turn right over a stile by a gate.

20. Walk along a fenced track. Just before a cattle grid in the track leading to Summerhill, go through a small gate. Follow the moorland path with a fence on the left. As you descend the moors you will see Tittesworth Reservoir in the distance. Eventually you will see Rockhall up to the right. Retrace your outward route back to the bus stop.

WALK 11
Castleton And Peak Forest

Castleton, Winnats, Sweetknoll, Peak Forest, Old Dam Lane, Oxlow Rake, Limestone Way, Cave Dale, Castleton.

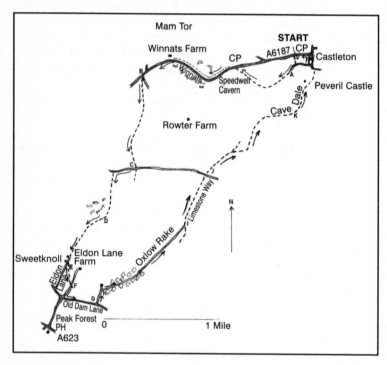

Maps: Explorer OL1 Dark Peak & Explorer OL24 White Peak.

Parking: Castleton SK149830

Linear distance: 7 miles

Approx. Time: 3 to 4 hours

Grade: 4★

Paths: Moorland paths and tracks and a rocky dale path

Stiles: SS

Refreshments: Castleton and Peak Forest

Picnic: Instructions 8, 14 & 16

Toilets: Castleton Visitor Centre and Speedwell Cavern Car Park.

Directions

The main car park in Castleton is by the Visitor Centre.

Description

This is a walk of contrast on which you will experience the dramatic Winnats pass, where the climb by the road is rewarded by the grandeur of towering valley sides. Gentle undulating moorland paths take you down to Peak Forest. The church there, at one time, was known to be the Gretna Green of the Peak. After walking up through parkland area near Oxlow Rake you reach the open grass moorland before descending steeply the dramatic Cave Dale with Peveril Castle towering above the lower slopes.

Route Instructions

1. From the car park in Castleton return to and cross the main road. Follow the Riverside Walk, a surfaced path, to the minor road and turn right. Cross the river bridge and walk up Goose Hill, first on a tarmac surface then a wooded stony track. {A}

2. Go through a gate to follow a path round the hillside, keeping a wall close on the right. You will cross one stile and gate. In about $1/2$ mile you reach the road.

3. Turn left passing the entrance to Speedwell Cavern. Walk up Winnats Pass by following the grass path on the right of the road. After about $1/2$ mile as you near the top of the Pass ignore a gate on the right and continue ahead up to and through a small gate, still following the road and now a wall on the left.

4. Just before the farm go through a small gate on the left. Continue in the same direction up the road passing the farm and the cattle grid. At a road junction keep straight on along the Sparrowpit road for about 75 metres. Ignore a ladder stile on the left then just past it turn left through a gate leading to Rowter Farm. {B}

5. Almost immediately leave the track to bear off right along a wide grass path.

6. Follow this path across the open rolling grassy moorland. Soon you will have a wall on the right, which you follow for about $1/2$ mile, crossing three stiles.

7. On reaching a gravel track turn right to cross a stile by a gate. {C} Ignore the stile on the left to continue along the track. In about 300 metres, at a footpath sign, turn left and go through a small gate signed "Public Bridleway".

8. Follow the walled and fenced path, ignoring the stile on the right, to go through another small gate. The route now bears right uphill to pass a wooden post. Continue along the grass bridleway with a wall and fence down on the left. Pass the rocky lime-

stone outcrops on the right, [picnic] then follow the wall and fence more closely as it bends round to the right. {D} As you descend the hillside cross a stile by a gate.

9. On reaching a shale track walk to and through a gate to continue down and passed Eldon Lane Farm and Sweetknoll.

10. Just passed the buildings turn left to go through a small gate and across a paddock. {E} Cross the stile then bear right across the field corner to go over another stile.

11. Walk diagonally across the next larger field aiming for a house near the bottom left hand corner. Cross a wall stile by a gate. {F}

12. Turn right down a shale track. At the road junction turn left. [If you need refreshment keep straight on down to the main road and The Devonshire Arms]

13. Follow Old Dam Lane for about $1/4$ mile to turn left by the Bridleway sign to Oxlow Rake. {G} Walk down the drive towards the farm and at the entrance turn right to cross a wall stile. {H}

14. Walk up the wide track through the grass covered mounds and open woodland. [This is a very pleasant area] In about $1/4$ mile, at the end of the trees, cross a stile by the left hand gate. Keep straight on with a wall on the left. In another $1/2$ mile go through a farm gate onto access land.

15. {I} Turn left to join the Limestone Way. Follow the wall on the left, which shortly goes round a right hand bend. Stay near the wall for about $1/4$ mile. Go through a gate and across a track to go over a stile by a gate opposite.

16. Walk up a short walled track going through a gateway. {J} At the Castleton sign bear right on a gradually descending grass path with Win Hill on the horizon. Go through two small gates following a well defined path between them. Continue ahead with a wall on the left to walk down Cave Dale. At a fork in the path keep straight on following the bridleway arrow. Pass through a small gate {K} [broken when this route was researched]. The dale now descends more steeply on a rocky path, which may have water flowing down it after heavy rain. As you near the end of the dale, with Peveril castle up on the left, the path opens out.

17. At the end of the dale cross a stile to walk down into Castleton. [Notice the plaque describing the origins of Cave Dale] At the road junction turn left to pass the war memorial on the right. Turn right down Castle Street passing the church on the right. At the T-junction turn left back to the car park.

WALK 12

Derwent Moor And Ladybower Reservoir

Cutthroat Bridge, Derwent Moors, Whinstone Lee Tor, Grindle Clough, Ladybower Reservoir, Ashopton, Cutthroat Bridge.

Map: Explorer OL1 Dark Peak
Parking: Cutthroat Bridge lay-by SK216874
Linear distance: 6 miles
Approx. Time: $2^1/_2$ to 3 hours
Grade: 2
Paths: Moorland paths and tracks and reservoir road
Stiles: S
Refreshments: Ladybower Inn [Instruction 14]
Picnic: Whinstone Lee Tor
Toilets: Inn

Directions

From Castleton take the A6187 to and through Hope. In 4 miles turn left on the A6013 to and through Bamford. At the reservoir T-junction turn right to follow the A57 for $2^1/_4$ miles passing over Cutthroat Bridge to turn right into the car park lay-by.

Description

On this walk you will be rewarded with superb views with very little effort. From Whinstone Lee Tor you can see the twin-peaks of Crook Hill and Win Hill, in the far distance is Losehill and Mam Tor, beyond the Edale valley is the Kinder Plateau. The relaxing walk along the side of reservoir brings you to what is left of Ashopton before the gentle climb back onto the moors and to the start of the walk at Cutthroat Bridge. It was named thus because in the 16th century a man was found fatally wounded in the face and throat. As these are grouse moors it is advisable to avoid the grouse-shooting season. [August and September]

Route Instructions

1. Turn left out of the layby to walk back down the busy A57 to cross the bridge. Turn right through a gate. {A}
2. Follow the main moorland bridleway, which soon bears round to the left. Follow the gentle climbing moorland route for about a mile.

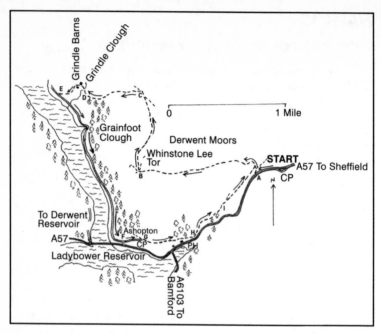

3. {B} At a crossing of six paths near Whinstone Lee Tor turn right to walk below the rock outcrops, staying on the bridleway.

4. Follow the path, with a wall on the left, for nearly a mile across the moors. About 100 metres before you turn left through a gateway another path comes in on the right.

5. {C} From the gateway walk down the moorland bearing slightly right and aiming for the top right hand corner of a conifer wood.

6. Pass through a gate and continue downhill with the conifer wood close on the left and a wall on the right. In about 300 metres turn away from the wood, you will now have a wall on the left. {D}

7. Go through a gate and walk down a rocky track to go through another gateway.

8. Cross Grindle Clough then pass through another gate [or gateway]. The route now takes you between barns before turning left to go through a small gate at the end of the barns.

9. Follow the stone slabbed path downhill at first with a fence on the right. At the bottom of the field go through a small gate. {E}

10. Turn left along the reservoir track. Cross Grainfoot Clough via a gate and a hairpin

bend. After walking about a mile along the reservoir road pass through a small gate.

11. {F} Take the left-hand road. Walk up the road passing the houses of Ashopton. At the end of the tarmac road keep straight on with the wood up on the left.

12. Pass through a gate and then a little further on pass through another gate ahead to enter the access land. {G}

13. Walk along a narrow undulating bracken-edged path, with the reservoir down on the right. Soon you will have a wall on the right.

14. Eventually pass through a metal gate to walk along a wider rather muddy path behind Ladybower house then Ladybower Inn.

15. {H} Join a wider track and turn left uphill to go through a metal gate to enter Ladybower Wood, the Derbyshire Wild Life Trust. Continue uphill on a wide stony track.

16. Where the path forks keep straight on following the "Bridleway and path to access land" sign. Continue ahead through the birch trees to pass under the power lines.

17. {I} Cross a stream to go through another metal gate. Follow the wide stony bridleway for about $^1/_4$ mile. As you near the end of this stretch you will see the road down on the right. At a fork of tracks near the power line poles bear right. Take care down the steep rocks to join your outward route. Turn right back to the main road.

WALK 13
Edale, Hope And Jaggers Clough

Edale Car Park, Hardenclough Farm, Hollins Cross, Lose Hill, Townhead, Hope, Fullwood Stile Farm, Guide Post Jaggers Clough, Nether Booth, Ollerbrook Booth, Edale.

Map: Explorer OL1 Dark Peak.
Parking: Edale SK 124853
Linear distance: 9 miles
Approx. Time: 4 to 5 hours
Grade: 4
Paths: Tracks and moorland paths
Stiles: S
Refreshments: In Edale and Hope
Picnic: Hollins Cross, instruction 6, Guide Post area, Jaggers Clough.
Toilets: Edale Car Park

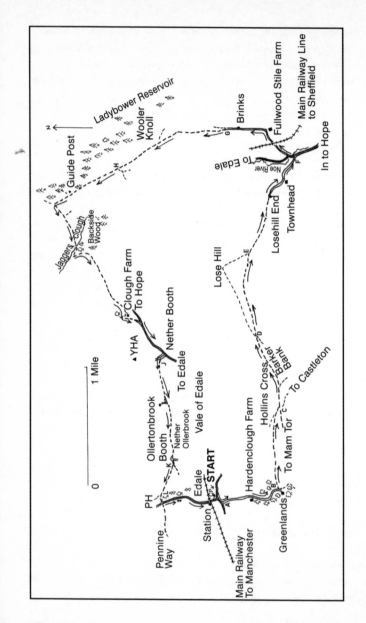

Directions

From Castleton drive westwards out of the town along the A6187 towards Speedwell Cavern then straight on to pass the cavern car park. Drive up the beautiful Winnats and at the road junction turn right. Go round a sharp left hand bend and in about $^1/_4$ mile turn sharp right to follow the signs to the car park at Mam Tor. Keep straight on uphill following the winding road which soon descends from Mam Tor to Barber Booth. Turn right for nearly a mile and just after the turn up to Edale turn left into the car park.

Description

If you have never walked in the Peak District then this walk is a must. As you walk you will have revealed to you the ridges, slopes, dales, rivers and woodlands that make up this awe inspiring countryside. There are some fairly long gentle climbs but the views are worth the effort.

Route Instructions

1. From the car park return to the road via the main vehicular entrance. Turn right passing the road up to Edale village. In another 100 metres turn left at the National Trust sign, Hardenclough Farm. {A}

2. Walk up the farm drive for about $^1/_2$ mile, passing Hardenclough Farm, to the gate across the drive into Greenlands. Just before this gate turn left by the Hollins Cross sign. {B}

3. Bear left to follow the Hollins Cross route on a fenced shale path which gradually climbs the hillside. You will pass through three gates. As you climb the route becomes more grassy and steeper. It should take about 20 minutes to reach the view point at Hollins Cross. {C}

4. Turn left up a wide stony track called Barker Bank along the top of the ridge ignoring a path off right and keeping a broken wall on the left. At the top of the climb go through a small gate. In about $^1/_2$ mile from Hollins Cross and opposite a stile on the left leave the ridge to turn right for a few metres where you join another path to turn left. {D}

5. Walk towards the trees where you pass through the right hand small gate. Follow the open woodland path contouring the hillside. Leave the wooded area via a stile.

6. Keep straight on along a wide undulating grass path across the hillside and cross four stiles. After the fourth stile, {E} below the path leading up to Lose Hill, turn right gradually veering away from the fence on the right. Stay on the wide grass path downhill,

51

the lower stretch of which is quite steep, aiming for a wall and fence ahead.

7. Follow this fence and broken wall on downhill. Go through a small gate to walk down a shady sunken path. Eventually cross a stile to turn left to walk down a track passing Losehill End Farm on the right. Continue down the surfaced lane.

8. At the T-junction at Townhead turn right to walk on down to the next road junction. {F} [If you need refreshments keep straight on along the Edale road to the Cheshire Cheese Inn, about 300 metres]

9. To continue the walk turn left to cross the bridge and keep straight on ignoring the Edale road on the left. Follow this surfaced lane, crossing the railway line, passing Fullwood Stile Farm at a left hand bend and continuing up the wooded Brinks Road. After passing Brinks go through a gate onto open moorland. {G}

10. Keep to the main wide stony and partly sunken track with a wall and fence on the left. As you near the top of this gradual climb the route becomes more open and undulating. After $^3/_4$ to 1 hour walking from the Edale Road you will cross a stile by a gate. {H}

11. Keep straight on, with the conifer wood over to the right, aiming for the guide post ahead. Pass the guide post [HOPE, EDALE, SHEFFIELD, GLOSSOP], go through the gate and walk up to the next gate ahead and cross the stile.

12. Turn left to follow the Edale route and keeping a fence on the left. Cross the stile ahead to keep straight on down a stony wide track ignoring a path off left.

13. As you near Backside Wood the track descends quite steeply into Jaggers Clough. Cross the stream to go through a small gate and turn right into the National Trust area. {I} Walk up the wide track which becomes quite steep after a left hand bend. At the top go through a kissing gate.

14. Continue to follow the track as it descends the hillside. Go through a gate. On reaching Clough Farm turn right at a T-junction of tracks to go through a small gate then across a small stream to walk behind Clough Farm. Follow the tree-lined path to the road.

15. Turn right for about 350 metres. Walk through Nether Booth to turn right at the Youth Hostel sign. Just before the cattle grid turn left through a small gate. {J}

16. Follow a wall then a fence on the right to go through two more gates. Join a track to continue in the same direction. Where the track turns up right keep straight on following a clear path then a track to go through 6 gates.

17. Pass Nether Ollerbrook going through a farm gate. The track now widens out and is fenced and walled. Through Ollerbrook Booth the track becomes a surfaced lane. Pass Ollerbrook Farm and holiday cottages. Follow the footpath signs to Edale Station.

18. At a left hand bend keep straight on through a small gate, {K} signed "Edale", to follow the yellow arrow signs. Walk through the farmyard passing the stables and bunk house. Go through two more small gates.

19. Now follow a track with a wall then a fence on the right. Go through a stile by a cattle grid and keep straight on.

20. At a fork of paths take the left hand path {L} to walk down a partly stepped cobbled path and going through gate then across a narrow bridge.

21. Walk up into Edale passing The Old Nags Head to turn left. Walk down through Edale for nearly $^1/_2$ mile passing the station to turn left back to the car park via the pedestrian entrance

WALK 14
Eyam, Stoke Ford, Great Hucklow

Eyam, Highcliffe, Stoke Ford, Oaks Farm, Abney Moor, Great Hucklow, Stanley Moor, Stanley House, Tideswell Lane, Eyam.

Maps: Explorer OL24 White Peak & OL1 Dark Peak
Parking: Eyam Car Park SK216767
Linear distance: 10 miles
Approx. Time: 5 to 6 hours
Grade: 4
Paths: Moorland and field paths and tracks near the end
Stiles: SSS
Refreshments: Great Hucklow and Eyam
Picnic: Stoke Ford & the end of Abney Moor
Toilets: Eyam Car Park

Directions

Eyam village is off the A623 Baslow to Peak Forest. Drive up the B6521 and at the top of the dale turn left. Drive through the village passing the church and the Hall. Turn right up Hawkshill Road to the pay-and-display car park.

Description

Eyam is well known as the plague village and you can see many references to it in the village. It was also the first village in the country to have piped water. In 1588 stone

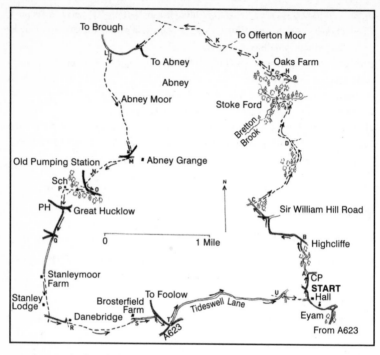

troughs were built to hold rainwater from the springs along the mile long street in the village. If you follow this very varied route in May you will be rewarded with a wonderful display of rhododendrons. The walk starts with a steep climb up Eyam Edge followed by more gentle undulating paths crossing moorland and valleys. The return route crosses farmland before following a wide track back to Eyam.

Route Instructions

1. From the car park turn right up the road. Where the road bends right bear left up a minor road, {A} The Nook, which shortly leads into a rough partly surfaced wide track winding uphill for about 1/4 mile.

2. On reaching the road at Highcliffe turn left. {B} Follow the road for nearly 1/2 mile and on reaching a wide track on the right [Sir William Hill Road] continue on the road round the left hand bend for another 30 metres then turn right down a rough track for just over 275 metres to a crossing of tracks. Turn right over a ladder stile by a gate. {C}

3. Follow the wide path keeping a wall close on the left and passing the large area of rhododendrons. After passing a small low building on the left leave the wide path to continue on up to the top corner of a wood and a stone gatepost.

4. Follow the wall and wood on the left crossing a stile by a gate, the grass path soon goes round a right hand bend. Cross another stile by a gate and turn left to continue following the wall on the left.

5. On reaching a gate in the corner of the moorland, cross the stile to the left of it and turn right. {D}

6. Follow a wide grass path along the ridge for about ¹/₄ mile crossing one stile. The path veers away from the wall on the right and descends in a curve down into Bretton Clough. Near the bottom of the slope the path divides into two, either path will take you to the path above the Bretton Brook.

7. Turn right along the path keeping the brook on the left. When you reach the bridge at Stoke Ford turn left down the bank to cross the bridge and a stile. {E}

8. Turn right to cross another bridge and in a few metres cross a stile just to the right to follow the Offerton Moor Oaks Farm route. {F} [NOT the Abney route]

9. Continue ahead up through the grassland then on up through the wood where the path becomes more obvious. Leave the wood via a stile to walk diagonally right up the field where you cross a stile by a gate.

10. Cross the road to go over another stile by a gate. {G} Walk up the wide chatter-covered drive. In about 150 metres bear off right, leaving the drive, to follow the footpath sign up a grass path. {H} At the top go over the stile and along a very short walled path to the farm track.

11. Turn right towards Oaks Farm. Just before the gate turn left up the grass path through the bracken. {I} Cross another grass path to keep straight on by the footpath post. During the summer this area of moorland is covered in bracken so it is important to keep to the paths.

12. Eventually you join a path coming in on the right near a wall corner. {J} Keep straight on up the moorland ignoring paths off left and right. At a junction with a wider grass path cross it diagonally left to keep straight on. The bracken starts to thin out and soon you will have a wall on the left, {K} which you follow for nearly ¹/₂ mile.

13. Cross a stile and continue ahead with a fence on the right and the wall on the left. Follow this wall where it bends round to the left by the footpath sign. Stay on the wide open moorland track for about ³/₄ mile passing the turn to Abney. Just after a right-hand bend in the track turn sharp left to cross a stile by the footpath post. {L}

14. Follow the wide open moorland path up and over Abney moor for about one mile.

There is a convenient picnic seat just before you reach the road.

15. Cross the stile onto the road and turn right. In about 100 metres and having gone round a bend, turn left and left again back on yourself to walk along a surfaced farm drive for a few metres to go through a small gate on the right. {M}

16. Cross the middle of the field to go through another small gate in the opposite corner. Follow the path down the steep field, cross a stream and on up the other side keeping a fence on the left. Go through a gated stile. Keep straight on down into a small valley, passing an old pumping station {N} and crossing a stream, then straight on up the two fields ahead going through two small gates

17. At the road turn left. After a left-hand bend and the end of a short stretch of railings turn right {O} then right again to pass the "Great Hucklow Wood" sign. Follow the concessionary path down through the wood. Ignore a gate and path on the left. Join the school drive and turn left. {P}

18. At the road junction turn left. [If you need refreshments turn right to **The Queen Ann** inn] Almost immediately turn right. Walk down the road and out of the village. At the road junction keep straight on along a fenced track. {Q}

19. At Stanleymoor Farm cross a stile on the left. Walk towards a stone barn crossing two stiles and fields. Pass the barn on your left and follow the wall on the right. Cross another stile by a large field gap. Follow the line of the telegraph wires passing Stanley Lodge on the right. Cross another stile and continue following the wall on the right to cross a stile on to the lane.

20. Turn left along the lane. At Stanley House keep straight on to cross a stile by the gate ahead. {R}

21. Follow the wall on your left to cross seven fields and stiles. [There is no wall on left in the 5th field] In the 8th field cross a stile in the field corner to join a farm track and turn right to the driveway. {S}

22. Walk along the farm drive passing Brosterfield Farm on the left. At the road junction turn left then right at the next junction. Just before the main A623 turn left down the wide stony track of Tideswell Lane. ["Unsuitable for Motors"] {T}

23. Follow the track for 1 1/4 miles. The track becomes a surfaced road as you enter Eyam. Turn right opposite the first bungalows on the left. {U}

24. Follow the path across the small field then across a track to walk down a fenced path between the houses to cross a road, continue down the wide pavement, then on down the road to the main village road. Turn left at the T-junction and in about 200 metres turn right up Hawkshill Road back to the car park.

WALK 15
Hartington And The Dales

Hartington, The Raikes, Narrow Dale, Wolfscote Dale, Biggin Dale, Dale End, Hartington.

Map: Explorer OL24 White Peak
Parking: Hartington SK128604
Linear distance: 8 miles
Approx. Time: 4 hours
Grade: 3
Paths: Field and dale paths and country tracks
Stiles: SSS
Refreshments: Charles Cotton Hotel also inns and tea rooms in Hartington.

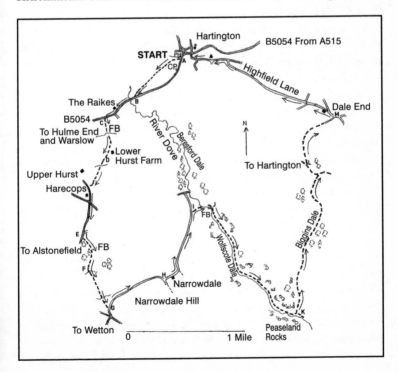

Picnic: Wolfscote Dale
Toilets: In Hartington

Directions

Hartington is 2 miles down the B5054 off the A515 Ashbourne to Buxton road about 10 miles north of Ashbourne. There is a small free parking area in the centre of the village and a pay and display car park a few metres down the Hulme End–Warslow road [B5054].

Descripton

Starting from one of the most typical of Derbyshire villages at Hartington, this walk will provide you with a good amount of exercise initially across undulating fields then down the limestone dales. Here you should feel the calm and peacefulness amidst a surfeit of beauty and grandeur.

Route Instructions

1. From whichever car park you use return to The Charles Cotton Hotel. With the hotel on your right walk up the B5054 Warslow road for a few metres and just before the Ceramics Works and Shop on the left, turn right at the end of a wall in front of a row of stone houses. {A}

2. Follow the wall and house wall to pass through a stone squeeze stile. Continue along a very narrow path between the buildings, then between a fence and a wall. Pass through a gate to pass a farm gate on the left. Follow a wall close on the left to cross another stile.

3. Keep straight on across the next five fields and stiles maintaining a southwesterly direction. In the fourth and fifth fields aim for a cottage and the road.

4. After the fifth stile walk to the B5054 {B} and turn right. Walk up the road for about 500 metres, passing into Staffordshire. Pass Raikes Farm on the right and the drive to Lower Hurst Farm on the left.

5. Just past the "Little Raikes Footpath" sign and the cottage on the left, turn left at the footpath sign. {C} Cross the stile and descend the field keeping a wall and fence on the left.

6. Cross a stile and footbridge to walk straight on up the next field. Go through a small gate.

7. Bear right up the field following the right hand direction arrow and aiming for a power line pole. Pass Lower Hurst Farm down on the left. Pass through a small gated stile in the field corner. Bear very slightly left to cross another wall stile by a water trough.

8. Bear slightly left passing a tennis court and keeping a fence on the left. {D} Go through a gate and across a stile to keep straight on, there are trees on the left and a steep bank on the right. Cross the fence and squeeze stile ahead [do not bear round to the right].

9. Walk up the next two fields aiming for farm buildings and crossing two stiles. Turn left along the road, passing Harecops Farm, then keep straight on at the crossroads following the Wetton and Alstonefield route.

10. In about 450 metres and after a track on the left turn left through a stile by a gate and the footpath sign. {E}

11. Continue ahead keeping a fence and the wood close on the right. Go through a small gate to continue following the fence then at the fence corner keep straight on to a waymarked post. Cross a planked footbridge.

12. Follow the hawthorn trees on the left for a short way, then bear right to cross a fence stile and footbridge. Bear right aiming for a large ash tree. Cross a fence stile just to the right of the ash tree.

13. Walk downhill crossing another fence stile and a marshy stream area, then bear left up the bank. At the top of the bank look for two old stone posts [once a squeeze stile] which are ahead and over to the left. Walk towards these stones through the reedy field. Cross a rather difficult fence stile by the stones and hidden by a hawthorn bush. {F}

14. Walk up the next field with a wall on your left for a short way and at the wall corner keep straight on aiming for the road signs on the horizon up ahead. Pass five large trees on the right and a ruined stone barn on the left. Walk down to and past a telegraph pole then on down the steep bank to cross a stream. Keep straight on up the steep field bearing slightly left aiming to the left of a farm gate. Cross the wall stile.

15. {G} Turn left down the minor road. Pass through a gate onto Access Land. Continue down the road round Narrowdale Hill. After about $1/2$ mile you go through a gate into the old farmyard of Narrowdale.

16. {H} **Turn left below the barn** to go through another two gates or gateways. Walk down the farm track to turn left.

17. Follow a gated track for about $1/2$ mile until you reach a small gate by a farm gate and a small gate up to the right, [new in 2007]. Turn right signed Hartington, to go through the small marked "Sabrina Way". {I}

18. Follow the new path then cross the River Dove via a gated bridge. Turn right through a stile. {J}

19. With the Dove on your right walk along the peaceful riverside path in Wolfscote Dale for $1^1/4$ miles.

20. {K} At the National Trust footpath sign turn left to follow the Biggin Dale route.

21. Walk up the gradually ascending dry and pretty Biggin Dale. After about another 1¼ miles you come to a footpath sign. Turn left to take the Hartington route.

22. Go through a small gate then turn right for about 200 metres and at the next footpath sign keep straight on to follow the route to Biggin.

23. Cross a wall stile to walk up the shallow dale for about ½ mile. At the road junction turn left.

24. In 100 metres branch off left between two houses in Dale End. {M} Walk up Highfield Lane and at a staggered crossing of tracks keep straight on following the Hartington route. 1½ miles from Dale End the track joins a road.

25. Turn left down the road passing the Youth Hostel. Follow the road round to the right to join the B 5054 into Hartington, turning left.

WALK 16

Hulme End And Butterton

Manifold Way Car Park, Warslow, Warslow Brook, Butterton, Villa Farm, Manifold Way.

Map: Explorer OL24 White Peak
Parking: Manifold Car Park Hulme End SK103593
Linear distance: 6 miles
Approx. Time: 3 to 3 hours
Grade: 2*
Paths: Field paths and tracks
Stiles: SSS
Refreshments: In Hulme End, Butterton and Hartington
Picnic: In the car park
Toilets: Near the car park

Directions

From Hartington take the B5053 to Warslow. In 2 miles, having passed through Hulme End village, turn left into the Manifold Car Park.

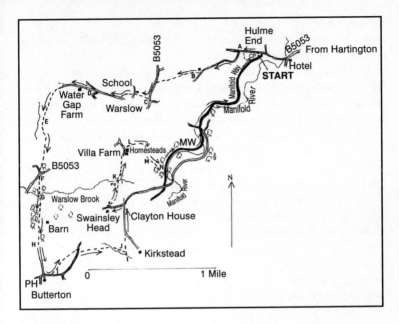

Description

This walk is best done after a period of dry weather in the spring or autumn when the grass is not so long. Except for one very steep climb of nearly 300 metres in just under ½ mile this is a pleasant walk across farmlands in the Peak District of North Staffordshire. The steep climb is rewarded with extensive views. Butterton has changed very little in the last 100 years.

Route Instructions

1. From the car park return to the road and turn left. In about 250 metres turn left immediately after Callow Farm. {A}

2. Follow the narrow minor road uphill for nearly ½ mile. Immediately after the first house on the right turn right up a short fenced area to turn left over the fence stile. {B}

3. Walk up the field, following the boundary on the left, to cross a squeeze stile ahead. Keep straight on in the same direction crossing four stiles and fields. [The third field is only across the corner of it] In the fifth field bear slightly right to go through a large gap then follow the fence over on the left aiming for the school up ahead. Cross

61

a stile by a gate.

4. Turn left along the B5053. In about 200 metres and just past the Warslow and 40mph sign turn right through a small gate. {C}

5. Keep straight on up the field with the boundary close on the left, ignoring a small gate on the left, aim for the farm barns ahead. Go through two farm gates and across a farm track to go through a small gate. Bear left up the field, keeping the hedge close on the left, to go through another small gate just before the field corner.

6. Follow a path through the rough area to the road opposite the converted chapel. Turn right to walk out of Warslow passing The Manifold Church of England School on the right. Just before the derestriction sign on the bend in the main road, leave the road to keep straight on along a gravel track. {D}

7. Stay on the main track to pass the renovated Water Gap Farm. The route now becomes a partly grassed track which shortly goes round a left hand bend before descending the hill where it can become overgrown in the summer. From the road to the track is about ¹/₂ mile. This track ends at a gate, so cross the stile by this gate. {E}

8. Walk down the field keeping the boundary on the right and passing a farm gate at right angles to your route. Continue to follow the fence on the right and a line of trees on the left. Cross a stile in the field corner.

9. Follow the field boundary on the left. Cross a stile near an old stone barn on your left and another stile to your right. Now continue following the field boundary on the left and just before the field drops almost vertically downhill turn left to cross the double stile. Keep straight on, still with the boundary on the left, to cross another double stile.

10. Turn left down the minor road to the T-junction and turn right along the B5053 for about 30 metres to go over a stile on the left. {F}

11. Keep straight on up the bank to cross another stile then follow the hedge and trees on the right. Near the bottom of the field follow a narrow winding path for a short way through the hawthorns to cross a footbridge, over Warslow Brook, via a stile. Climb the bank ahead.

12. {G} The next part of the walk is not so obvious as this area is very steep ahead and undulating on either side. Aim to stand facing uphill with the footbridge at your back and slightly to the right. Keep straight on up the very steep slope with a deep tree filled gully on the right. As you near the top you will see a ruined stone barn over to the left then a fence up ahead. Look for a gate in the fence which should be over to the right.

13. Cross a stile by the gate and keep straight on. {H} Soon you will have a line of

trees on the left then a fence and wall, where you follow a farm track. Cross a stile by a gate and follow the track which leads into Butterton.

14. On reaching the village road turn left. [If you need refreshments turn right to the "Black Lion"] Walk along the road for about 100 metres, passing the church, to turn left through a stile. {I}

15. Bear right across the field to go through a squeeze stile then walk diagonally across the next field to go over a stile hidden in the field corner. Cross the bottom of the third field to go through another stile. Now cross the left hand corner of one field and the right hand corner of the next field via two stiles.

16. Bear slightly left, away from the wall, to cross the field. Cross a gated stile onto the road. Turn right for about 25 metres then turn left to cross a stile by a gate.

17. Follow the hedge on the right to the bottom of the field. Cross a stile and a footbridge by the telegraph pole and to the right of a farm gate [or gateway]. Keep straight on to cross two more small fields and stiles. In the third field bear left down to and across a small footbridge and a fence stile.

18. Turn right to follow the stream down on the right. Cross the stile ahead and pass an old stone barn up to the left. Keep straight on to the hawthorn hedge ahead. Ignore an old squeeze stile and turn left. {J} Follow this hedge on the right as you walk up the field. Pass an old small gate and stile on the right to keep straight on across the middle of the field.

19. Cross a stile to join a track and turn left. Walk along the track, crossing a stile, to the road. Turn left up the road for about 200 metres. Cross a wall stile on the right opposite Swainsley Head farm and by a barn.

20. Walk between the barn and the field boundary then bear left down to the telegraph pole. Go through the small gate ahead. Bear left down to the bushes which are to the right of a farm gate. Continue in the same direction aiming for the lowest telegraph pole near the bottom of the field. Pass this telegraph pole on your left and bear right to descend the steep bank under the trees.

21. {K} Cross the gated footbridge, ignoring the blue bridleway sign, bear right up to the top right hand corner of the field. Go through a small gate and walk up the bridleway.

22. Go through another small gate to follow the "Alternative Footpath" route round the gardens of Villa Farm. Cross a cattle grid and immediately go through a stile by the Lower Homesteads gate. Keep straight on round the back of Homesteads to cross a stile by a farm gate. {L}

23. Continue ahead up the field to go through a squeeze stile. Bear right across a marshy

area, partly on duck boards. Cross two old stiles in the marshy area to bear right across the next marshy field corner. Cross the stile.

24. Walk towards an old stone barn to cross a stile below it. {M} Bear left to walk downhill to have a hedge on the left. Cross a stile ahead then turn left through a hedge gap to turn right and continue in the same direction through the wood.

25. The path soon descends quite steeply on a partly stepped path down to the Manifold Way via a stile by a gate.

26. {N} Turn left signed Warslow. Follow the surfaced track for about 1¹/₄ miles back to the car park.

WALK 17
Wetton And The Manifold Way

Wetton, Wetton Hill, Manifold Way, Weag's Bridge, Beeston Tor Farm, Larkstone Lane, Castern Wood Nature Reserve, Wall Ditch, Wetton.

Map: Explorer OL24 White Peak
Parking: Wetton car Park SK 109552
Linear distance: 6¹/₂ miles
Approx. Time: 3 hours
Grade: 3★
Paths: Moorland, dale and field paths, tracks and minor roads
Stiles: SSS
Refreshments: The Royal Oak in Wetton
Picnic: Instruction 13
Toilets: At Wetton Car Park

Directions

From Hartington take the B5053 Warslow road and in 1¹/₂ miles turn left by the hotel in Hulme End. Follow this road for another 1¹/₂ miles and at Gateham Grange take a narrower road on your right. Stay on this minor road going round a left-hand bend then a shallow right-hand bend, ignoring a road off left to go round another sharp right-hand bend and continuing into Wetton village. At the T-junction in the village, opposite The Royal Oak, turn left to follow the parking signs.

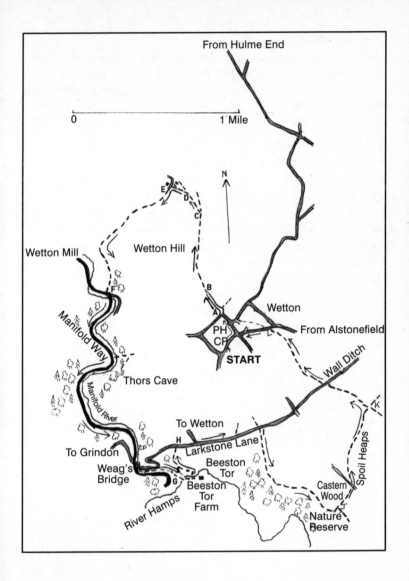

From Hulme End

0   1 Mile

N

E
D
C

Wetton Hill

Wetton Mill

B
A
Wetton

Manifold Way

PH
CP
START

From Alstonefield

Thors Cave

Manifold River

Wall Ditch

To Wetton

H
Larkstone Lane

To Grindon

Weag's
Bridge

G
Beeston
Tor

Beeston
Tor Farm

Castern
Wood

Spoil Heaps

River Hamps

Nature
Reserve

65

Description

A walk of contrasts from the quiet stone built village of Wetton. The easy route between the high rounded Wetton Hills gives fine views of the Staffordshire White Peak before a peaceful stroll down the dale between the hills to join the busier, flat, surfaced Manifold Way. The return to Wetton gives you a chance to climb some quite steep hills before walking above the impressive Manifold Valley.

Route Instructions

1. From the car park turn left down the road and at the T-junction turn left again to walk up through the village ignoring roads off to the right and passing The Royal Oak. Where the road bends left bear right up a wide surfaced lane. {A}

2. Follow this lane ignoring the stile on the right, and shortly passing a reservoir installation on the right. {B} Go through the gate then through the squeeze stile ahead.

3. Follow the path up round the hill to go through another squeeze stile.

4. Keep straight on across the hillside. Soon you will see a barn down on the left and a stile in the fence at the bottom of the hill. Cross this stile and keep straight on aiming for the wall over on the left, to cross a stile in the field corner.

5. Keeping the wall close on your left continue down the field and at a wall corner turn left still following the line of the wall. {C} At the next fork of paths bear left {D} the wall is on the left. As you approach a house ahead bear off right to cross a footbridge and a stile.

6. Turn left below the house to go through a gate onto the access land. {E}

7. Follow the gradually descending dale path for about $^3/_4$ mile. Cross the stile by a gate at the bottom of the dale. {F}

8. At the junction with the Manifold Way keep straight on to cross the wide wooden bridge. [If you need a light refreshment stop at Wetton Mill turn right for about $^1/_4$ mile]

9. Walk along the flat Manifold Way to Weag's Bridge, $1^1/_4$ miles. After passing the car park cross the minor road by the bridge to take the left-hand track.

10. Follow the track with the dry Manifold Valley still on the left. Walk passed the caravan site to cross a footbridge over the Hamps River then cross a stile. {G} Continue along the partly surfaced farm track towards Beeston Tor Farm. In a few metres, before reaching Beeston Tor Farm, turn left at a footpath sign to go through a gate.

11. Walk down a path and across the dry riverbed, or if wet follow the stepping stone sign. Cross a stile onto the "National Trust Beeston Tor" land. [Notice the magnificent limestone cliffs of Beeston Tor]. Walk up the short steep bank to the footpath sign.

Turn left up a wide fairly steep grass path by the gorse. [Wonderful views] Cross a stile by a gate and turn right to follow a wall on the right and the line of an old wall on the left.

12. Cross a stile onto the minor road and turn right up Larkstone Lane {H} for nearly $^1/_2$ mile and at the bottom of the hill turn right through a squeeze stile to follow the Castern and Highfield Mine route. {I}

13. Keep straight on to cross another stile then bear right up the field aiming for a wall corner then keep straight on to cross a wall stile to the right of a water trough.

14. Walk above the Manifold Valley for about $^3/_4$ mile, you will cross one stile and after going through a small gate turn up left, {J} to cross a wall stile by the Castern Wood Nature Reserve.

15. Continue ahead to follow a track with a wall close on the left and old spoil heaps on the right. At the tall metal footpath post cross two stiles and a track to follow the Hopedale route. Bear left across the field to go through a stile.

16. Keep straight on crossing four fields and keeping a wall close on the left. In the fourth field, where the wall bends left continue ahead to cross a wall stile in the field corner. Cross the next field to a small gate and footpath sign. [Do not go through the gate] {K} Turn left signed "Wetton". Walk diagonally back up the same field to cross a stile near the top left-hand corner.

17. Bear slightly away from the wall on the right to cross a stile. Walk diagonally across the next larger field aiming for trees near the top left-hand corner. Cross a stile, the road [Wall Ditch] and another stile then a small gate.

18. Bear left up the field crossing a stile then keep straight on towards the trees passing a waymarked post. Follow the hedge and then a wall on the right to cross a stile. Continue in the same direction crossing three fields and stiles. Go through a small gate onto the road. {L}

19. Turn left up the road back into Wetton and at the road junction turn right then left to follow the car park signs.

WALK 18

Offerton Moor And Derwent Heritage Way

Hathersage, Leadmill, Mount Pleasant, Callow Wood, Offerton Hall and Moor, Shatton Lane, Brough Lane, Townfield Lane, Shatton, Derwent Heritage Way, Stepping Stones, Hathersage.

Map: Explorer OL 1 Dark Peak
Parking: Hathersage SK232814
Linear distance: $9^1/_2$ miles
Approx. Time: 5 hours
Grade: 3
Paths: Riverside, woodland and moorland paths and tracks
Stiles: SS
Refreshments: In Hathersage or two short detours to The Travellers Rest on the A6187 [an extra $^1/_2$ mile] or the garden centre near Shatton [an extra 100 metres]
Picnic: Offerton Moor, the start of Brough Lane, Derwent Heritage Way
Toilets: In the centre of Hathersage reached via a path at the bottom right hand corner of the car park

Directions

Park in the main Hathersage Car Park which is a few metres up the secondary road linking the B6001 and the A6187.

Description

A pleasant and stimulating walk especially in mid-spring when the bluebells in Callow Wood are delightful to see. The bracing moorland paths and tracks eventually lead down to the Derwent Heritage Way where you follow the riverside path to the large stepping stones across the Derwent River. If after prolonged rain these 500-year-old stepping stones are flooded you will need to continue along the riverside to Leadmill then retrace your outward route back to Hathersage.

Route Instructions

1. From the car park return to the road and turn right down to the B6001, turn left and in a few metres turn right down Dore Lane. Walk under the railway bridge and on reaching the entrance to Nether Hall at the bend in the road turn left over the stile by the farm gate, signed "Leadmill Bridge. {A}

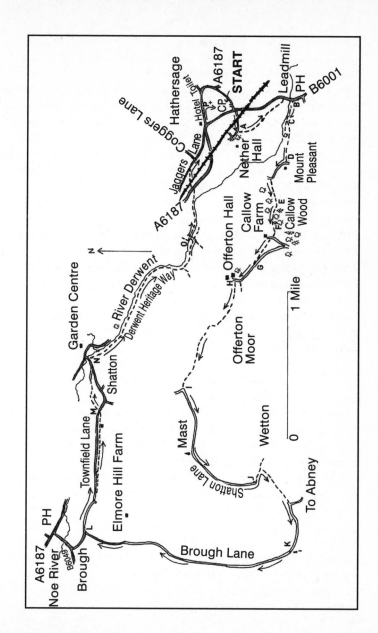

2. Follow the farm drive then a path, keeping the fence on your right and crossing stiles, to reach the B6001. Turn right across the river bridge then immediately turn right again through the wall and over the stile. {B}

3. Follow the riverside path for about 200 metres and just passed a derelict barn and by an old stile turn left away from the river. {C} Follow a line of old posts across the field to climb up a short steep wooded bank [the twisting path is the easier climb]. At the top cross a wall stile.

4. Turn right to follow a wall, fence and the wood on the right. At an old stone gate post and stile head up the field aiming for a farm gate. Go through a small gate by this farm gate on to the minor road at Mount Pleasant. {D}

5. Turn sharp right down a farm track signed "Broadhay Farm". In about 250 metres turn left through a gate at the footpath signs.

6. Walk up the field and under the power lines, turn left to follow the power lines for a few metres before veering away from them up onto a banked grass track that leads to a small gate. Go through the gate into Callow wood. {E} Follow the wide woodland path that soon bears up right heading for a wall at the edge of the wood. Eventually leave the wood via a small gate. {F}

7. Bear slightly left up the field to go through a stile and small gate. Walk up the farm drive to a gateway going through and immediately turning right to walk behind Callow Farm.

8. Stay on the well defined path which soon descends a small valley via a stile. In another 200 metres cross a stile onto a minor road and turn right. {G} Pass Offerton Hall down on the right and at a sharp right hand bend walk towards a farm gate with the Open Access sign. Cross the stile to the right of this gate, [or go through the gate]. {H}

9. Follow the bridleway with a wall on the right, gradually ascending Offerton Moor, for about $^3/_4$ mile. As you come over the brow of the hill walking away from the wall, aim for a farm gate. Go through this gate. {I}

10. Turn left up Shatton Lane, which soon becomes a gravel track, aiming for the high mast ahead. Stay on this lane for about a mile and then go through a gate. Turn left along a stony track signed "Abney and Brough". Follow the track round the hillside and on reaching a footpath post keep on round to the right. {J}

11. Follow the rutted track with a wall close on the left. Pass a road on the left, signed "Abney" and keep straight on still with the wall on the left. Follow this main track round to the right, you are now on Brough Lane. {K}

12. Continue down Brough Lane for nearly $1^1/_2$ miles. It becomes very stony and rocky as you descend, but the last $^1/_4$ mile is surfaced.

13. At a sharp left hand bend turn right on to a track. {L} [If you wish to visit The Travellers Rest turn left into Brough where you will turn right]

14. Follow the track uphill crossing two stiles by two gates. Pass through a third gate to follow a track round a field with a wall then a hedge on the right. Go through a farm gate on the right onto Townfield Lane.

15. Turn left for about 75 metres, then right onto a wide path above the lane that you follow, ignoring the point where it joins the lane. At a footpath sign keep straight on to walk behind a converted stone barn and shed keeping the lane down on the left.

16. Go through a small gate and over a stile. Follow the field boundary on the left to go through another small gate and down steps. Cross the lane to go up steps and over a stile. {M}

17. Keep straight on crossing three fields and stiles. Walk down the road in Shatton for a few metres and at the T-junction turn left. Just before the bridge and the main road turn right over a stile. [If you wish to visit the garden centre keep straight on to the main road]

18. {N} Follow the clear path, cross a footbridge and continue along the undulating Heritage Way riverside path for about $1^1/_4$ miles. You will pass through a number of small gates and cross two footbridges.

19. On reaching a footpath post turn left down the river bank to cross the stepping stones over the Derwent River. {O} Climb the bank and turn right to continue following the river, now on the right.

20. In nearly $^1/_4$ mile and having crossed a stile bear left, away from the river, up to a small gate.

21. Pass through the gate and cross the busy A6187 to go over a stile then up a narrow field and over a ladder stile. Take great care when crossing the main railway line. Walk diagonally right up the next field to go through a small gate. Turn right down Jaggers lane. In about $^1/_4$ mile join the main road to walk into Hathersage. At the toilets cross the road to walk up the church drive {P} then along a fenced path to the car park.

WALK 19

Stanage Edge And Redmires Reservoir

Dennis Knoll Car Park, Long Causeway, Stanage Pole, Redmires Reservoir, A57, Surrey Farm, Crawshaw Lodge, Moscar Lodge, Stanage Edge, Dennis Knoll.

Map: Explorer OL1 Dark Peak
Parking: Dennis Knoll SK 228844
Linear distance: 9 miles
Approx. Time: 4 to 5 hours
Grade: 4
Paths: Moorland and stony edge paths with some boggy areas

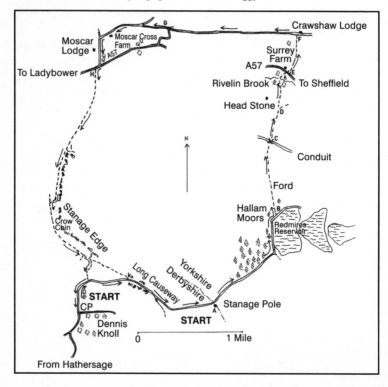

Stiles: S

Refreshments: In Hathersage about 2 miles away

Picnic: By the reservoirs and at instructions 7 and 12 [the outcrop of rocks]

Direction

From Hathersage take the A6187 Hope road. Just after passing The George Hotel turn up right along Jaggers Lane. In about 300 metres turn right up Coggers Lane. [See map for Walk 17] Where the road forks take the left fork and continue on up the minor road crossing a cattle grid to reach the small car park at Dennis Knoll.

Description

This high level walk starts with a 1¹/₂ mile gradual climb on a wide stony causeway [possibly of Roman origin] up onto the gritstone moorland of Stanage Edge to reach Stanage Pole on the Derbyshire/Yorkshire boundary. A gradual descent on an old stone flagged path then a forestry track brings you to the Redmires Reservoirs. From here 1¹/₄ miles of undulating moorland paths lead to the A57 and a rather steep climb up to Crawshaw Lodge. [A reasonably good picnic stop with wonderful views on a clear day] After following a secondary road with good views [about 1 mile] and a wide track, the route returns to the car park via a spectacular walk along Stanage Edge the first part of which could be boggy in places.

Route Instructions

1. Leave the car park to follow a wide stony and rocky track. As you near the top of the Long Causeway ignore a path off right and stay on the main track until you reach Stanage Pole, 1¹/₂ miles from the car park in about ³/₄ hour. {A}

2. At the pole continue along the main stone slabbed track. Pass through a gate to walk down to the reservoirs on a wide shale track.

3. At the reservoirs stay on the track, as it bends round to the left, to join a surfaced road. Just after the first bend by the reservoirs turn left at the footpath sign to go through a small gate. {B}

4. Walk up a wide walled path to go through a small gate on to the moors.

5. Continue up the moorland keeping a wall close on the right. The path shortly descends a small valley where you cross a planked path to go over a stile. Continue on up the moorland path still with the wall on the right. At a wall corner keep straight on and soon you will see parts of a broken wall on the left.

6. Cross a bridge over the conduit then cross the stile ahead. {C} Follow the path as it descends the moorland. At a waymarked post {D} keep straight on noticing the Head

Stone over to the left. As you aim for the main road ahead take care as this section of the descent path has been worn down to a small gulley.

7. Cross the A57 and turn right for a few metres to go over a stile by the public footpath post. {E} Walk up the next two fields passing Surrey Farm on the left and go through two stiles. Continue ahead to follow a path which goes first through the reeds and then winds up steeply through scrubland. Cross a stile and bear right to join the road. {F}

8. Turn left to follow the road for about a mile. Where the road bends sharp left keep straight on along a wide track going through a gate. {G} Stay on this rough walled track for about $3/4$ mile passing Moscar Cross Farm and going through farm gates or gateways.

9. When you reach a wall ahead turn left down a wide grass track passing the boundary stone and Moscar Lodge. At the junction with the A57 turn right for a few metres then turn left at the footpath sign. {H}

10. Walk up to and over the stile onto the moorland. Follow the moorland path [sometimes rather boggy] as it gradually climbs up to Stanage Edge. In about $3/4$ mile you will see the large gritstone outcrops of Stanage Edge, at this point ignore a path off left going through the Edge. {I} Keep to the path just below the high rocks up on your left. Shortly the path bends right downhill to a T-junction of paths where you turn left. Continue on this path with the impressive Crow Chin rocks up on the left.

11. As you continue along this route the views across to Win Hill and Kinder plateau are very commanding. You will also see a number of millstones in the heather slopes. Eventually you will see ahead the causeway you climbed at the start of the walk.

12. There are two paths off right, take the second of these which is just after an exceptionally large millstone [without the centre hole] on the right-hand side of the path and opposite a smaller fully cut millstone. {J}

13. Walk down the hillside aiming for and crossing the ladder stile. Turn right to retrace your outward route.

WALK 20

Peter Dale And Miller's Dale

Miller's Dale, Tideswell Dale, Tideswell, Wheston, Peter Dale, Wormhill, Monsal Trail.

Map: Explorer OL24 White Peak
Parking: Miller's Dale Monsal Trail SK139732
Linear distance: 8¹/₂ miles
Approx. Time: 4 hours
Grade: 2
Paths: Field, tracks and dale paths
Stiles: SS

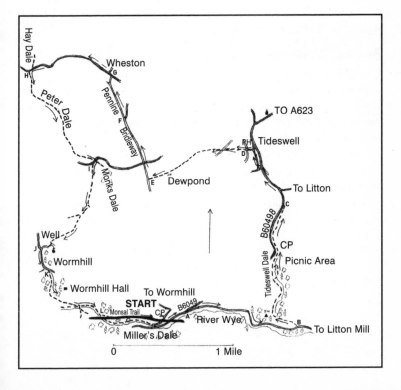

Refreshments: Miller's Dale and Tideswell
Picnic: Peter Dale and Tideswell Dale
Toilets: Monsal Trail and Tideswell Dale car parks

Directions

From Tideswell take the B6049 south to Miller's Dale. Drive through Miller's Dale and about 250 metres after passing under the bridge turn right up the Wormhill road. Almost immediately after passing under another bridge turn left into the Monsal Trail car park.

Description

A very varied walk across the fields and dales west of Tideswell, where there are wide open views and deep secluded limestone dales. Spring is the best time for this walk when Peter Dale is a riot of wild flowers. If you wish this walk could start at instruction 4 in the Tideswell Dale car park. The 14th century parish church of St John the Baptist – "Cathedral of the Peak" is worth a visit.

Route Instructions

1. Leave the car park via the main entrance and turn right down the road and under the bridge. At the junction with the B6049 turn left to walk through the village passing under the bridge again. In about 500 metres bear off right to follow the pretty minor road to "Litton Mill only". [Notice the enclosure on the right where you can read up the history of the area] {A}

2. Pass the "Anglers Rest" and continue along the road for about a mile. Just before the "No public parking at Litton Mill" notice and by a lay-by turn left signed "Tideswell Dale". {B}

3. Walk up the interesting gently sloping dale for a mile. You will go through one gate and at a bridge you can turn right or go straight on as the two branches of the brook side path meet ahead.

4. Walk into and through the car park and picnic area. Near the road entrance on the left keep straight on along a tree lined path. At the end of this path go through a small gate.

5. Follow the road and wall on the left. When you reach a fence ahead go through a small gate on the left to cross the road. {C}

6. Walk up into Tideswell. In just over ¼ mile and at the start of the village, pass Richard Lane on the left. Turn left up steps by the bus shelter. At the road turn right.

7. Follow the narrow village road [Thorncliffe Terrace] down towards the main road.

Just before "The Horse and Jockey" turn left up the steep narrow Primrose Lane.

8. Cross the road diagonally right to go through a stile by a farm gate. {D}

9. Walk up three fields, crossing through three stiles and keeping a wall close on the right. Cross a track diagonally to go over the stile. Keep straight on still with the wall on the right. Cross four fields and stiles. In the fifth field bear left over a stile then continue ahead crossing three more fields and stiles [the third field is very narrow].

10. Keep straight on down the middle of the field aiming for a wall corner and passing a dew pond on the left. Cross the wall stile ahead and keep straight on up the next field with the wall now close on the left. Cross the stile in the field corner. {E}

11. Turn right along the track. At the road junction keep straight on following the "Pennine Bridleway".

12. In just over ¼ mile keep straight on where the minor road bends right, {F} still on the "PBW". In another ¼ mile turn left to walk through the hamlet of Wheston.{G}

13. Follow the descending minor road for just over ½ mile, ignoring a road off right. At the bottom of the hill, where paths cross the road, turn left signed "Miller's Dale". {H}

14. Walk down through the varied scenery of Peter Dale. After nearly a mile pass the Monks Dale notice board and shortly afterwards you will cross the stile onto the road.

15. Turn right for about 75 metres then turn left through a stile. {I}

16. Climb the steep hillside aiming for, then following, an old wall, hawthorns and a fence on the left. Pass a waymarked post then go through a gate or stile. Follow a walled path gradually uphill. When you meet a wall ahead turn right to continue uphill on a grass path, in about 175 metres cross a stile by a gate and immediately turn left over another stile.

17. Follow the wall on the left. Shortly you will enter a walled track. At the end of this track keep straight on through a kissing gate.

18. Carry on across the middle of the field aiming for the farm and farm gate. Turn left by the farm gate to cross the stile.

19. Follow the short winding path to go through a gateway by the church, notice the Helm Tower. Turn right to follow the church road to the T-junction of roads in Wormhill.

20. {J} Turn left along the road and in about 400 metres, at the decontrolled sign, leave the road to walk down a track on the right. {K}

21. Pass a cottage on the left then go through a gate to walk down the woodland path.

As you leave the wood keep straight on along the higher grass path. Soon you will bend round to the left before gradually descending the valley side. The lower limestone rocky slopes can be quite slippery after heavy rain.

22. In the valley bottom go through a small gate and turn left to follow the River Wye on your right. Just before the viaduct turn sharp left up the steep stone steps to the Monsal Trail. {L} [At this point you could continue along the riverside path to the road then turn left back up to the car park]

23. Turn left along the trail passing the impressive old lime kilns. In about $^1/_2$ mile you will be back at the car park.